# Universal Design
# for Learning in Action

# Universal Design for Learning in Action

## 100 Ways to Teach All Learners

by

**Whitney H. Rapp, Ph.D.**
St. John Fisher College
Rochester, New York

·P·A·U·L·H·
BROOKES
PUBLISHING CO.®

Baltimore • London • Sydney

**Paul H. Brookes Publishing Co.**
Post Office Box 10624
Baltimore, Maryland 21285-0624

www.brookespublishing.com

Typeset by Auburn Associates, Inc., Baltimore, Maryland.
Manufactured in the United States of America by
Bradford & Bigelow, Newburyport, Massachusetts.

Cover images are ©istockphoto-GlobalStock, ©istockphoto-AVAVA, ©Getty Images/Blend Images.

Selected photos are copyright © 2014 Jupiterimages Corporation.

The individuals described in this book are real people whose situations are based on the authors' experiences.
Real names and likenesses are used by permission.

**Library of Congress Cataloging-in-Publication Data**

Rapp, Whitney H.
 Universal design for learning in action : 100 ways to teach all learners / Whitney Rapp.
  pages   cm
 Summary: "Need creative ideas for moving UDL from theory to practice? Get this must-have quick guide,
ready for any teacher to pick up and start using now. Whitney Rapp, co-author of the acclaimed Teaching
Everyone, walks you step by step through 100 UDL strategies that strengthen student engagement, learning, and assessment. Based on the latest research (but still practical and fun!), these highly effective ideas
will help you address diverse learning needs and increase all students access to the general curriculum.
Essential for every educator who wants to know what UDL really looks like, sounds like, and feels like and
how to use this proven approach to teach and reach all learners. 100 UDL STRATEGIES FOR: Classroom
space and materials: The best uses of seating, lighting, bulletin boards, and more   Classroom management:
From smoother schedules and meetings to effective transition areas   Technologies: Fresh ways to use blogs,
videoconferencing, e-books, and more   Content instruction: Teach academic content with tools like music,
drawing, mnemonics, and humor   Social interaction: Creative games and small-group activities that
sharpen all kids social skills   Executive functions: Great ideas for templates, rubrics, graphic organizers,
timers, and web-based materials   Transition to adulthood: Prepare students for the real world with charts,
goal plans, and more   Assessment: New ways kids can show what they know from adapted tests to family
projects"—Provided by publisher.
 Summary: "Easy-to-understand and implement strategies for teaching using universal design for learning
to reach all learners"—Provided by publisher.
 Includes bibliographical references and index.
 ISBN 978-1-59857-390-9 (paperback)—ISBN 978-1-59857-514-9 (epub3)
 1. Inclusive education—United States.  2. Teaching—United States.  3. Universal design.  I. Title.
 LC1201.R37 2014
 371.9′0460973—dc23                                                    2013049478

British Library Cataloguing in Publication data are available from the British Library.

2018

10   9   8   7   6   5

# Contents

**Section V    Strategies for Assessment**

**Section VI   A Living Resource**

# About the Author

**Whitney H. Rapp, Ph.D.,** Associate Professor of Inclusive Education, St. John Fisher College, 3690 East Avenue, Rochester, New York 14618

Dr. Rapp is Associate Professor of Inclusive Education at St. John Fisher College, where she teaches courses on inclusive education pedagogy, assessment, classroom management, and diversity issues. Dr. Rapp holds a bachelor's degree in elementary education and psychology from the State University of New York at Potsdam and master's and doctoral degrees in special education from Michigan State University. Prior to her experience in teacher education, Dr. Rapp taught many grade levels in a variety of settings, from fully inclusive classrooms to residential special education schools. All of these experiences reinforced her belief that all children can learn and that all children should learn together in inclusive settings. Dr. Rapp's current research interests include universal design for learning throughout the school years and college. She is the coauthor of the textbook *Teaching Everyone: An Introduction to Inclusive Education* (coauthored with K.L. Arndt; Paul H. Brookes Publishing Co., 2012), and she presents at local, state, national, and international conferences on differentiation of instruction, teacher education, and inclusion. She serves on the Board of Directors of TASH. Dr. Rapp's spare time is spent with her husband and three children, riding bikes, hiking, playing board games, reading, watching movies, and enjoying Owasco Lake.

# Acknowledgments

I owe great thanks to many people who made this book possible:

*My family*—my husband, Steve; my children, Sam, Oliver, and Vivian; and my parents, Carol and George. Thank you for your unwavering support and patience with me and my grandiose ideas (e.g., writing two books in 2 years).

*All of the teachers, students, and professionals who shared their ideas and classrooms with me*—Camaron Clyburn, Maggie Driscoll, Liz Fyles, Beth Jackelen, Steve Jacobs, Jamie Nells, Cassie Pruitt, Shawn Ranney, Rob Rice, Chris Simmons, Benny Smith, and Laurence Sugarman. Thank you for your invaluable contributions.

*The fantastic folks at Brookes Publishing*—Rebecca Lazo, Steve Plocher, and Janet Wehner. Thank you for your expert advice and interest in my work.

*The wonderful writing retreat women*—Katrina Arndt, Lisa Cunningham, and Jill Swiencicki. Thank you for reviving my creativity and nourishing my writing soul.

*My "students"*—Bridget, Caroline, Connor, Elise, Greta, Luke, Oliver, Pierce, Sam, Vivian, and Wilkes. Thanks for your help!

*For Steve Rapp, nobody else in the world*

# Overview

# FOUNDATIONAL THEORIES

There are so many pedagogical theories out there, including universal design for learning (UDL), understanding by design (UbD), differentiated instruction (DI), culturally responsive teaching, brain-based research, and full citizenship. Which is the best one? Which is the most effective? Which one do I follow? The answer is all of these. At the heart of all of these theories is a solid belief in the strengths and abilities of all students and an unwavering commitment to create classrooms that belong to everyone equally, all the time. The overview of this book describes each of these theories, explains why effective teachers must follow them all, and describes how they all fit together for truly inclusive practice.

The sections that follow are the heart of the book, with dozens of concrete applications of each UDL principle to propel the reader into action. Each strategy presented includes a strong rationale for its use, modeling the thinking and planning that is necessary before applying the strategy. All of the strategies are teacher tested, most can be implemented immediately, and they are intended to be of use to anyone. All teachers, even those well familiar with the concepts and theories presented, can benefit from more ideas of what these theories look like, sound like, and feel like in practice.

As a whole, this book operationalizes full inclusion—the theory, attitudes, and beliefs, plus practical ideas, strategies, and applications. You must have all of these in place for learning to truly be for all. A feeling of belonging and community in a classroom is as essential as the curriculum taught there. Each student deserves to feel comfortable in the classroom from the start—that he or she is as important and valuable and accepted as anyone else. Planning ahead should account for all of the students equitably, and even though we cannot predict everything and some adjustments will always be necessary, the adjustments should happen for everyone equitably as well. This book gives you theory and practice, sending you on your way to create a classroom that is universally designed for learning. In other words, one that is truly inclusive and truly effective.

This section explores the theory of UDL and how it intersects with DI, UbD, brain-based research, full citizenship, and culturally responsive teaching.

## Universal Design for Learning

The National Center on Universal Design for Learning (2011) defined UDL as a set of principles to follow when developing a curriculum so that the curriculum meets the needs of every student, giving all students equal opportunities to learn.

As outlined in the Higher Education Opportunity Act of 2008 (PL 110-315), UDL provides flexibility in the ways information is presented, the ways in which students respond or demonstrate knowledge and skills, and the ways in which students are engaged. UDL reduces barriers in instruction and provides appropriate accommodations, supports, and challenges. It also maintains high achievement expectations for all students, including students with disabilities and students with limited English proficiency.

***Why Universal Design for Learning?***    The purpose of UDL is to meet the needs of all students in an inclusive classroom. Students are vastly diverse—in *what* they learn (what they perceive), *how* they learn (how they process), and *why* they learn (what interests and motivates them). If a curriculum is designed with a single "average" student in mind, it will exclude more students than it includes because students learn in many different ways. No two students are alike in their thought processes, learning styles, abilities, and interests.

The National Center on Universal Design for Learning (2011) described traditional curricula as having "curricular disabilities" because they only are designed for "average" students and thus fail to meet the needs of real classrooms, in which not every student is "average." These curricula present the content in one or two ways that are accessible to certain students, but they offer limited instructional options.

A UDL curriculum identifies all the different ways a curriculum needs to be customized so that it can be accessed by all students. Addressing what, how, and why students learn, and understanding what each student would report about what he or she learns, empowers educators to create classrooms in which all students are full citizens. It also empowers educators to advocate for students so that their needs are met in all settings.

An important distinction must be made here. UDL is not the same as retrofitting (making after-the-fact adaptations to) a traditional curriculum. Rather, UDL is a process by which a curriculum is purposefully and intentionally designed right from the start to address diverse needs (National Center on Universal Design for Learning, 2011). This is a philosophical distinction as well as a technical one. The practice of retrofitting means that some students (typical students) were thought of first, and other students (those who need adaptations) were thought of later. It sends the message that the classroom is made for only some, and others need to be worked in.

UDL is also valuable because it fosters the development of expert learners. Expert learners understand how they learn best and thus do not just receive content but create ways to gain access to content according to their unique needs. These students show that they are resourceful and knowledgeable by activating their own background knowledge to lend it to the learning situation; identifying and using tools and resources for gaining access to new learning; and transforming unfamiliar knowledge into meaningful, useful knowledge. These students show that they are strategic and goal-directed by making plans for learning, organizing effective resources and strategies to be used, and recognizing their own strengths and weaknesses. These students show that they are purposeful and motivated by setting their own challenges, sustaining the effort and persistence needed to achieve the goals, and monitoring their own interest levels and progress toward goals.

### *Principles of Universal Design for Learning*
There are three primary principles of UDL as originally outlined: 1) provide multiple means of engagement, 2) provide multiple means of representation, and 3) provide multiple means of action and expression (National Center on Universal Design for Learning, 2011; Rose & Meyer, 2002).

#### *Provide Multiple Means of Engagement*
The first principle for designing a curriculum based on UDL is to use many different ways to engage students in learning. Everyone becomes engaged by different types of tasks and different learning situations. Some students prefer working alone, whereas others prefer group work. Some prefer open-ended, highly subjective tasks, whereas others prefer structured, objective tasks. Each student is unique in his or her learning style and abilities, and in the ways he or she engages in various learning opportunities. To increase engagement, teachers need to catch students' interest and help them sustain effort, persist toward a goal, and self-regulate their learning behaviors.

#### *Provide Multiple Means of Representation*
The second principle to follow when designing a curriculum based on UDL is to provide multiple ways of representing the content to be learned. Rapp and Arndt (2012) described this as *input.* If you provide the content in just one way, only the students who can gain access to it that way are going to benefit from it.

If you present it in multiple ways, three things happen: 1) more students are going to have access to the new learning, 2) the new information will be reinforced in multiple ways, and 3) students will be more likely to be expert learners because they will be familiar with multiple ways to receive information and thus will know what works best for them so that they can explore a range of ways to learn new information.

*Provide Multiple Means of Action and Expression*   The third principle to follow when designing a curriculum based on UDL is to provide multiple ways of action and expression. Rapp and Arndt (2012) described these ways for students to show what they know as *output*. The two most common traditional outputs are writing (e.g., tests, worksheets, essays) and oral responses to teacher-posed questions in class. Although these methods should be continued for the students who are well able to demonstrate their learning in these ways, many more options need to be offered as well. To meet the output needs of all learners, options for physical action, communication, and executive functions (i.e., different ways for organizing, planning, and executing tasks) are essential.

Closely related to providing multiple means of expression, it can be helpful to consider a fourth principle: *Provide multiple means of assessment.* This fourth principle is not part of the original concept of UDL but was proposed by Rapp and Arndt (2012) as an additional consideration. Ways in which teachers evaluate students must vary along with the ways in which students are engaged in learning, materials are represented, and students represent what they know. Areas explored under multiple means of assessment are formal and informal assessment, formative and summative assessment, and alternative assessments (see Section V).

## Universal Design for Learning and Self-Advocacy

The practice of UDL does not just help students learn in the here and now to get them through each grade. If implemented effectively, it also prepares all students to have ownership of their learning and progress and to advocate for themselves and for each other. Experiencing multiple means of engagement, input, output, and assessment, and having the opportunity to reflect on those experiences affords students the knowledge and skills to be self-reliant, lifelong learners.

In elementary school, teachers implement universally designed curriculum and space to support all students in their learning of the K–5 content. At the same time, in kindergarten through second grade, students begin to learn about themselves as learners. Teachers support them in exploring their learning styles, needs, difficulties, and preferences. Teachers create a climate that encourages sharing of successes and failures without shame or blame. In Grades 3–5, this development of self-knowledge continues as students experience even more ways of learning.

In middle school, teachers implement universally designed curriculum and space to support all students in their learning of the sixth- to eighth-grade content. The students are also learning study skills and organizational skills that will support them in high school. By this time, they are now knowledgeable about themselves as learners. They have developed passionate interests and are familiar with their strengths and difficulties. Now is the time to help them voice that knowledge to others who are involved in their learning (e.g., teachers, parents, peers).

In high school, teachers implement universally designed curriculum and space to support all students in their learning of the 9th- to 12th-grade content, as well as their future in the community, workplace, and/or higher education to prepare them to be college and career ready. At the same time, students continue to develop their self-advocacy skills until they are experts at advocating for their needs and future goals.

An environment that is universally designed for learning includes everyone and prepares everyone to be inclusive and think inclusively. It shows students that everyone is different, everyone has strengths, and everyone has needs, and that is okay. It shows students there are multiple ways to be successful, multiple ways to solve problems, and multiple ways to learn from mistakes. This is the most important learning because these students will be the adults in each other's lives. They will be each other's colleagues, supervisors, mentors, and supports. The more universal and inclusive classrooms are, the more universal and inclusive communities and workplaces will become because that will be what we all know best. Eventually, that will be the "way we have always done it."

 **Two must-reads on universal design for learning are**

Nelson, L.L. (2014). *Design and deliver: Planning and teaching using universal design for learning.* Baltimore, MD: Brookes Publishing Co.

Rose, D.H., & Meyer, A. (2002). *Teaching every student in the digital age: Universal design for learning.* Alexandria, VA: Association for Supervision and Curriculum Development.

## Understanding by Design

UbD is deliberate and focused instructional design driven by whatever it is students should come to understand. As Wiggins and McTighe summarized

> Our lessons, units, and courses should be logically inferred from the results sought, not derived from the methods, books, and activities with which we are most comfortable. Curriculum should lay out the most effective ways of achieving the specific results. It is analogous to travel planning. Our frameworks should provide a set of itineraries deliberately designed to meet cultural goals rather than a purposeless tour of all major sites in a foreign country. In short, the best designs derive backward from the learning sought. (2005, p. 14)

It is important to consider that understanding is not the same as knowledge. McTighe and Wiggins (1999) outlined six facets of understanding as the ability to 1) explain, 2) interpret, 3) apply, 4) have perspective, 5) empathize, and 6) have self-knowledge. Rather than create an activity and steer it toward a particular end, backward design of instruction and curriculum thinks first of the desired facet(s) of understanding and works backward until the lesson is complete. The three steps in backward design are to identify the desired results, determine the acceptable evidence, and plan learning experiences and instruction (McTighe & Wiggins, 1999). In doing so, students will think differently about their role in learning. Rather than thinking about learning as the activity itself, they will be able to understand that learning comes from the meaning behind the activity (Wiggins & McTighe, 2005).

## Differentiated Instruction

DI is the practice of understanding individual students' needs and adjusting instruction to match those needs to maximize student learning. In order to do this, teachers need to be comfortable in the disciplines they teach, flexible in their pedagogical methods, and proficient in knowing their students as individuals (Tomlinson, 2003).

Differentiation means knowing each of your students well. The purposes of differentiation are to ensure that students are each being challenged with work that is challenging but not too difficult and to help each student become an independent learner. Wormeli stated

> The two simple charges of differentiation are 1) do whatever it takes to maximize students' learning instead of relying on a one-size-fits-all, whole-class method of instruction and 2) prepare students to handle anything in their current and future lives that is not differentiated, i.e., to become their own learning advocates. (2007, p. 9)

Members of the classroom need opportunities to become a community. This is important for the teacher as well as fellow students. The teacher needs to know each student's likes, dislikes, experiences, and dreams. The teacher also needs to know each student's strengths and challenges in academics, behavior, communication, and physical development. In addition to establishing a community from the first day of school, it is important to assess your students both formally and informally to know where they are functioning so that attainable goals are set for everyone. If the student has an individualized education program (IEP), past assessment results and annual updates about his or her present levels of performance should be reported. Information from the IEP is useful, but it is important to remember that students' skills and knowledge change more often than the information on the IEP is updated.

Differentiation strategies and ideas are often simple: allowing a student to tell a friend the answer rather than writing it down, spelling words in sand or shaving cream rather than on paper, using large writing utensils or a pencil grip on standard-sized writing utensils, allowing a little more time to finish, and/or providing choices for projects or homework. You do not need a specialist degree to implement any of these strategies—just the proper mind-set, a desire to think outside of the box, and flexibility.

### Integrating Understanding by Design and Differentiated Instruction

In their book *Integrating Differentiated Instruction and Understanding by Design: Connecting Content and Kids,* Tomlinson and McTighe (2006) masterfully integrated these two important concepts. One cannot occur without the other. If UbD is the *what, when,* and *how* to teach, then DI is the *who* and *how.* As the authors so aptly stated, "In tandem, UbD and DI provide structures, tools, and guidance for developing curriculum and instruction based on our current best understandings of teaching and learning" (Tomlinson & McTighe, 2006, p. 3).

Seven axioms define this integration (Tomlinson & McTighe, 2006):

1. The primary goal of quality curriculum design is to develop and deepen student understanding.

2. Evidence of student understanding is revealed when students apply knowledge in authentic contexts.

3. Effective curriculum development following the principles of backward design helps avoid the twin problems of textbook coverage and activity-oriented teaching in which no clear priorities and purposes are apparent.

4. Regular reviews of curriculum and assessment designs, based on design standards, provide quality control and inform needed adjustments.

5. Teachers provide opportunities for students to explore, interpret, apply, shift perspectives, empathize, and self-assess.

6. Teachers, students, and districts benefit by "working smarter" and using technology and other vehicles to collaboratively design, share, and critique units of study.

7. UbD is a way of thinking; it is not a program.

### A few must-reads on understanding by design and differentiated instruction are

Tomlinson, C.A. (2003). *Fulfilling the promise of the differentiated classroom: Strategies and tools for responsive teaching.* Alexandria, VA: Association for Supervision and Curriculum Development.

Tomlinson, C.A., & McTighe, J. (2006). *Integrating differentiated instruction and understanding by design: Connecting content and kids.* Alexandria, VA: Association for Supervision and Curriculum Development.

Wiggins, G.P., & McTighe, J. (2005). *Understanding by design* (2nd ed.). Alexandria, VA: Association for Supervision and Curriculum Development.

Wormeli, R. (2007). *Differentiation: From planning to practice grades 6–12.* Portland, ME: Stenhouse Publishers.

## Culturally Responsive Teaching

Gay (2010) defined culturally responsive teaching as using the cultural knowledge, experiences, perspectives, and styles of ethnically diverse students to teach to and through the strengths of students, making learning more relevant and effective. Culturally responsive teaching is validating and affirming, comprehensive, multidimensional, empowering, transformative, and emancipatory.

Culturally responsive teaching is validating and affirming in that it bridges meaningfulness between home and school by acknowledging the legitimacy of and praising cultural heritages. By using a variety of instructional strategies, resources, and materials, teachers can be responsive to diverse learners. If students learn subject matter through a range of instructional methods, in an array of groupings, and with various modalities, positive self-concepts develop because culturally based learning styles are acknowledged and understood.

Culturally responsive teaching is comprehensive in that is encompasses every learner. Each student is valued and celebrated for who he or she is and what he or she brings to the setting. The expectation of a culturally responsive classroom is that everyone is responsible for the success of each individual member of the community. Successful, culturally responsive classrooms embrace the belief that all students have the right to be part of a mutually supportive group.

Culturally responsive teaching is multidimensional in that all aspects of the learning environment are involved. The curriculum, context, classroom climate, student–teacher relationships, pedagogy, and assessments recognize the diversity of the learners by tapping into a wide range of cultural knowledge, experiences, contributions, and perspectives. Teachers in different disciplines (e.g., language arts, math, science, history) can collaborate to teach a particular concept. Students can help decide how their progress will be evaluated while being accountable for many cognitive and collaborative skills.

Culturally responsive teaching is empowering through high expectations for students to succeed in an environment that recognizes cultural differences and effective pedagogical practices that respond to those differences. Providing resources and supports, combined with encouragement and a philosophy of achievement, push students toward academic competence, personal confidence, courage, and the will to act. In such environments, students are the source and center, consumers, and producers of knowledge.

Culturally responsive teaching is transformative because it confronts and transcends the cultural hegemony that resides in curriculum content and instruction of traditional education, and it develops social consciousness, critique, and efficacy. It recognizes strengths and accomplishments rather than focusing on failures and weaknesses. It affiliates diversity with achievement to deflect learned helplessness.

Last, culturally responsive teaching is emancipatory because it liberates students to find and use their own voices, examine issues through multicultural perspectives, engage in thinking, and become active participants. It carries away the notion that there is one truth and brings forth the freedom to reclaim the many different ways to be and learn.

Cultural differences are assets. When differences are present, students not only have the opportunity to learn about other cultures but they also have the opportunity to learn about issues stemming from cultural differences, such as racism, prejudices, stereotypes, injustices, and oppression. They have the opportunity to gain skills needed to build relationships with others, speak up against prejudices and injustices, and become change agents.

### Two must-reads on culturally responsive teaching are

Gay, G. (2010). *Culturally responsive teaching: Theory, research, and practice* (2nd ed.). New York, NY: Teachers College Press.

Nieto, S. (2013). *Finding joy in teaching students of diverse backgrounds: Culturally responsive and socially just practices in U.S. classrooms.* Portsmouth, NH: Heinemann.

## Brain-Based Research

An important area in the field of education is research on the brain and associated learning processes. Neuroscientists are finding out much more information about the brain—how it learns, how it forms new pathways and connections, how awareness is heightened. This is essential information for educators as they build inclusive classrooms.

What we know about brain plasticity is that neurons in the brain, most of which are present at birth, continue to grow throughout our lives with each new experience. The neurons actually sprout new dendrites, or branches, for each new bit of information to form pathways (Willis, 2006). So, the more ways that we experience or learn something, the more pathways that are built in our brain. Once the pathways are formed, frequent use makes them stronger and more efficient.

As Willis (2006) noted, "cells that fire together, wire together" (p. 7). If several different pathways have been connected to a certain topic or memory, they will all be activated together. The more pathways that are connected together, the more efficient the retrieval and flow of information. Over time, triggering the beginning of a pathway ignites the whole network. So, our job as educators is to introduce learning brains to a myriad of ways to learn something. More pathways!

The National Research Council presented a broad overview of brain-based learning research on the following key findings:

1. Students come to the classroom with preconceptions about how the world works. If their initial understanding is not engaged, they may fail to grasp the new concepts and information they are taught.

2. To develop competence in an area of inquiry, students must have a deep foundation of factual knowledge, understand facts and ideas in the context of a conceptual framework, and organize knowledge in ways that facilitate retrieval and application.

3. A metacognitive approach to instruction can help students learn to take control of their own learning by defining learning goals and monitoring their progress in achieving them. (2000, pp. 14–18)

To this end, teachers must draw out and work with their students' preexisting understandings, teach some subject matter in depth with many examples, and teach metacognitive skills. Classroom environments must be designed to be learner centered, knowledge centered, formative assessment centered, and community centered (National Research Council, 2000).

### Some must-reads on brain-based research are

Jensen, E. (2005). *Teaching with the brain in mind* (2nd ed.). Alexandria, VA: Association for Supervision and Curriculum Development.

Jensen, E. (2008). *Brain-based learning: The new paradigm of teaching* (2nd ed.). Thousand Oaks, CA: Corwin Press.

National Research Council. (2000). *How people learn: Brain, mind, experience, and school.* Washington, DC: The National Academies Press.

Willis, J. (2006). *Research-based strategies to ignite student learning.* Alexandria, VA: Association for Supervision and Curriculum Development.

## Full Citizenship in the Classroom

Belonging to a community of learners who value each other's strengths and challenges is an important part of being a citizen in the classroom. In addition to building a classroom community, teachers also must meet the academic needs of all students in the classroom. What does it mean to be a *full citizen* academically as well as socially? In the book *Schooling Children with Down Syndrome: Toward an Understanding of Possibility*, Kliewer (1998) outlined the following four elements of citizenship: 1) a belief in one's ability to think, 2) a belief in one's individuality, 3) a belief in the reciprocity of the relationship, and 4) a shared social place.

*A Belief in One's Ability to Think*   Everyone is capable of thinking—thinking deeply, thinking creatively, thinking for him- or herself. To achieve this, educators must broaden the way they think about thinking and intellect. Disability and intellect, for instance, are not mutually exclusive. It is just as likely for a person with a disability to have a particular gift as it is for someone who does not have a disability. Many believe that having a disability is actually what makes it possible to have a gift. Sometimes, unique ways of processing and functioning in the environment are defined as a disability. These unique ways of processing and functioning may also open the doors for achievements not accessible to those who process or function in typical ways.

*A Belief in One's Individuality*   Each person has unique characteristics. Even though a person may belong to a certain group, for example, it does not mean that he or she is exactly like everyone else in the group. This is particularly an issue with people who share a disability classification or label. Each person with a disability is a unique person, but labels construct assumptions that everyone who falls under the same label is alike. Not everyone with an intellectual disability is the same any more than everyone who is the same height is the same. Just like a signpost on a road, a label can point us in a general direction, but we will not know the details of a place until we go there ourselves, spend time, and make our own discoveries. To realize each student's full citizenship, it is essential to believe that each student is an individual.

*A Belief in the Reciprocity of the Relationship*    On an individual level, believing in the reciprocity of the relationship means that you believe that everyone has something to give and everyone has something to receive; everyone is a teacher and a learner. On a classroom level, it means that no one student or group of students enhances the classroom whereas another student or group of students drains it. In essence, everyone equally benefits and challenges the community. Working through the challenges benefits everyone because it helps them build problem-solving skills, persistence, and self-reflection. Also, the community is stronger for everyone when a problem has been solved.

Students with disabilities are often thought of as the receivers and their peers without disabilities as the givers. In fact, one of the loudest arguments against inclusive education is that it might be good for the students with disabilities, but it would not be fair to the students without disabilities. In this book, I explain how the opposite is true if one believes in the reciprocity of the relationship. Diverse people are better off when together, otherwise we are all deprived of experiences and opportunities to learn, make new friends, and grow as people ourselves.

*A Shared Social Place*    The idea of the shared social place brings together all of the concepts of citizenship. It is a place where each individual belongs, is valued, and can take risks without fear of failure or persecution. Once you have this in place, you are ready to also learn ways to differentiate lessons and activities to nurture the academic growth of all students.

*What Happens When All Students Are Not Full Citizens?*    When differentiated classrooms are not realized, there are many scenarios that could take place instead. It may be that students with disabilities are segregated into separate classrooms or separate schools and marginalized as second-class students.

The marginalization can be significant and overt or mild and subtle, but if it exists, full citizenship will not occur. In turn, effective differentiation toward academic success will not be likely. Students who experience this marginalization repeatedly are at risk of developing self-esteem and self-worth problems. They are more likely to become detached from teachers and parents, have behavioral challenges, skip or drop out of school, and become involved in substance abuse (Morrison & Cosden, 1997; Rodis, Garrod, & Boscardin, 2001). It is important to understand what makes a student a full citizen, but it is also important to know what marginalizes a student so that you can always be working toward a classroom in which all students are learning together in a community and in which everyone is valued and assumed to be a competent, contributing member (Miller, 2006).

### Some must-reads on citizenship in the classroom are

Kliewer, C. (1998). *Schooling children with Down Syndrome: Toward an understanding of possibility.* New York, NY: Teachers College Press.

Sapon-Shevin, M. (2007). *Widening the circle: The power of inclusive classrooms.* Boston, MA: Beacon Press.

Sapon-Shevin, M. (2010). *Because we can change the world: A practical guide to building cooperative, inclusive classroom communities.* Thousand Oaks, CA: Corwin Press.

Schwarz, P. (2006). *From disability to possibility: The power of inclusive classrooms.* Portsmouth, NH: Heinemann.

## HOW DO ALL OF THESE FOUNDATIONAL THEORIES FIT TOGETHER?

As mentioned previously, all of these foundational theories need to come together in truly inclusive classrooms in which learning and the environment are designed for all students. How is that possible? Consider the Venn diagram in Figure 1.1. Each circle represents one of the foundational theories. See how each of the circles overlap a little bit with each other? There are ideas embedded in each of these theories that make them similar to each other. For example, UDL and brain-based research both discuss ways that learners and their brains are best engaged in tasks and the importance of establishing multiple means of exposure to new content. UbD and DI blend the *what* to teach with the *who* to teach. UbD and culturally responsive teaching both focus on the discovery of students' prior understanding and the creation of authentic contexts for learning. DI, culturally responsive teaching, and the concept of full citizenship all focus on the individual—interests, strengths, and needs. Finally, UDL and the concept of full citizenship emphasize the importance and value of a shared place—a learning community that is for everyone.

Looking back at the circles, you will see how each one has its own space where it does not overlap at all. Each of these theories also has its own unique concepts that are not

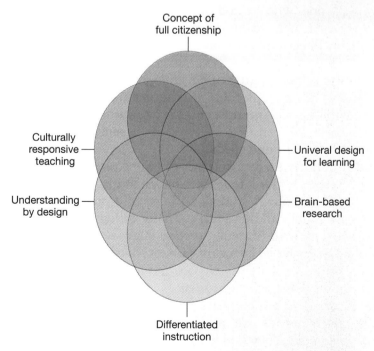

**Figure 1.1.** The foundational theories overlap like the circles in this Venn diagram.

shared by the others. As a group, they encompass all of the important elements, but no one theory embodies them all.

Now look at the very center of the diagram where all of the circles overlap. This is the essence of this book. These theories are unique, but when they all come together, they form the essential core of full inclusion: All students are important; all students can learn; all students deserve the best opportunities and the best their teachers have to offer. You will read this over and over in this book. It may seem repetitious at times. It felt repetitious to write at times. That is because it cannot be said enough. It bears repeating. *All* means *all*. Every way for everyone.

## WHAT DOES THIS BOOK ADD TO ALL OF THESE THEORIES?

This was an important question for me to ask myself as I worked on this book. The authors of the must-reads listed in the previous sections are incredible and have had such a positive impact on the field with their contributions; how could I possibly say it any better? Well, in many ways I cannot, but I am pulling these giants together to show that many heads are better than one. So, when I indicate that a book is a must-read, I really mean it. You must read it. The authors' ideas are so wonderful, so important, I could have rewritten all of their thoughts and ideas right over again. Instead, I chose highlights to include in this book to create a balance, and I send you off to the library or bookstore in search of the books you must read!

There are other points that I hope to drive home in this book. They are things that I have pulled together over the years from the work of other theorists, working with other teachers, bonding with other parents, and raising my own children. I believe in them with my heart and soul, and I parent, teach, and learn with them in mind.

First, *ability* and therefore *disability* are socially constructed concepts. We have, as a society, decided over time what makes someone able and what makes someone less able. Because we are the ones who created these definitions, we can be the ones to change these definitions. It is time to change our definition of [dis]ability.

Second, I truly believe that we have no right to sort humans into categories and label them. People are too complex, too dynamic, too unique to be pigeon-holed, and for that reason, classification systems are not effective in the education of our youth. No matter how we sort people into groups, there will be as much diversity, if not more, within each group as there will be across groups. Our job as educators is to meet our students' needs. Needs are not labels. We cannot sort by needs because there are no two people in the world who have the exact same needs.

Third, I do not think there is one theory or one program or one strategy that is most important. I do, however, think that there is one attitude that all teachers must have. Let me start with this anecdote. A student once asked a professor, "How will I ever be able to teach a whole class of children with so many different needs?" The professor, my esteemed colleague Dr. David Rostetter, replied, "It may sound corny, but the answer is to love them all." By *love them all*, he meant care for them all like they are your own, like your sole job in the world is to be their advocate and to do as much as you can for all of them. You must believe that every single student is as important and deserves as much of you as any other student. You must believe that every student can and will learn and has the right to any supports needed. Not all students are easy to teach. Some will exhaust you and keep you up at night. They will worry you, aggravate you, and sometimes even scare you. They will also thrill you and surprise you and teach you. That is why I am in this and why I think all teachers should be in this. If all students were easy, teaching would be boring. Give me the challenge. Give me a problem to solve. Give me all of them. But then stick close by because I will need you and your great ideas, too.

## ADDRESSING BARRIERS AND MISCONCEPTIONS

In working with teachers in various settings, I have heard several arguments against using UDL. This section relays the arguments and explains why they are misconceived.

### This Takes Too Much Time

Yes, it may take more time to set up a universally designed classroom and plan a universally designed curriculum. It takes longer to search for materials that engage students with diverse learning styles, cultural backgrounds, and unique needs. The question is not whether or not it takes more time, the question is What is *too much* time if it means engaging and reaching every student, and thereby improving outcomes for all?

### It Is Too Much to Ask Teachers to Do

Yes, it is a tall order. However, the more time and effort teachers invest in meeting the needs of all students from the onset, the more time they will save in the long run. It is not too much to ask teachers to invest in every single student. It is not too much to ask teachers to value every single student. A classroom is only as good as the child it does the least for. We should be doing the most for everyone.

### We Do Not Have Resources for a Universal Design for Learning Specialist

Every teacher is already a UDL specialist. UDL or any of the other theories are not areas of advanced specialty or programs that require intensive training. They are principles to follow and mind-sets to use when planning daily practices. Sometimes resources are needed in order for teachers to engage every student, ensure that every student can access materials and information, and provide ways for every student to demonstrate learning. Time and cost is a concern for many teachers. Districts have limited budgets, and it is commonplace for teachers to spend money out of their own pockets to stock their classrooms. Some of the strategies in this book are free or inexpensive. Others are highly technical and cost money or require some training. All are meant to be reasonable for the opportunity they provide to teach all students.

### This Is Not the Way We Have Always Done It

Nope, and for good reason. The way we have always done it is not working. With only 40% of U.S. fourth graders and 35% of U.S. eighth graders proficient in math and only 34% at those grade levels proficient in reading (National Assessment of Educational Progress, 2011), we need to approach teaching and learning of diverse learners differently. Rather than imposing testing and programs on the masses, we need to teach to individuals.

### Universal Design for Learning Is Just a Passing Trend

Many programs have come and gone in schools and classrooms for many different reasons. Perhaps they were not cost effective. Perhaps they were too open-ended or too prescriptive. Perhaps they did not fit the mission or values of the school. Rather than being a program, UDL is a set of principles to follow, a way of thinking when developing plans and instructional methods under any program or set of standards. UDL is a match for any school that values inclusion and success for all of its students, which is not a passing trend.

## Universal Design for Learning Means "Anything Goes" in the Classroom

To some extent, maybe anything should go in the classroom if it means a willingness to think outside of the box and try anything to make a difference in engaging students, while providing multiple means of input, multiple means of output, and multiple means of assessment. If, however, you consider the negative connotation of *anything goes* to mean any performance level is acceptable, any behavior is acceptable, or little to no progress is okay, then the concepts of this book do not mean *anything goes*. A very important consideration for each strategy is whether high expectations are met for all students. The content, knowledge, and skills are not watered down—they are made accessible to all students. The expectations are not lowered—all students are supported in reaching them.

## I Already Differentiate for the Few Who Need It; What Is the Difference?

There are two big differences. One, there are not just a few students who need it. Thinking that way perpetuates the idea that there is one main way to learn with a few who deviate from that way and need extra help. In fact, every single student needs differentiation, in some way, at some time, for something. Second, universally designing learning goes beyond the basic concept of differentiating. To employ a differentiated reading strategy for Mary and a differentiated math strategy for Juan is great for Mary and Juan and may help them significantly in reading and math, but it is shortsighted. Both the reading strategy and the math strategy need to be available for all of the students in the classroom.

## That Is a Lot to Do for Just One Student

There are two responses to this. First, as in the previous answer, it is not just for one student. It may be one student with a particular need that brought that strategy to light, but if it is put in place, many others will benefit. There is always a ripple effect. Second, even if it is just one student who needs it and it is a lot to do, do it. The student is worth it.

## Doesn't This Mean that Some Students Will Have an Unfair Advantage?

Actually it means that some students will stop having an unfair *dis*advantage. It means that all students will have a *fair* advantage. I used the following analogy in an IEP planning meeting once to illustrate the idea of leveling the playing field and equitably supporting each student.

Compare going to school with going on a hike. Everyone has to make the hike. The hike is long. Each and every kid makes the hike with his or her backpack of baggage. Now imagine that every difficulty a student experiences is a rock in his or her backpack. A few students go the distance with very little difficulty because the environment matches their needs. These kids have no rocks in their backpacks, or maybe just little pebbles. Most kids encounter some amount of difficulty along the way, not because they are less able but because there is a mismatch along the way. A student is deaf and very few people in the school use American Sign Language (ASL)—big rock. She is still on the hike, still moving forward, but she is carrying a rock that no one else is carrying. A student has difficulty integrating all of the sensory stimuli in the classroom, and there are only overhead fluorescent lights—big rock. A student has difficulty managing all of the materials, handouts, and assignments that are expected in a day of high school and none of his teachers post information on a web site to access later when he is at home doing homework—big rock. UDL strategies do not excuse students from the hike, nor do they carry them on the hike, nor do they shorten the hike. UDL strategies take the rocks away (or at least trade them in for little pebbles).

## Where Is the Set of Strategies Proven to Work?

There is no set of strategies to use together as a prescribed program, nor is there a guarantee they will work with all students. And nor should there be. To guarantee that a strategy or even a set of strategies works with all students assumes that all students are alike in some way. This book is based on the conceptual framework that all students are unique, and many different things need to be in place to work for all of them. The strategies are presented with a research base or strong theoretical foundation as sound ideas to start with if you feel they are a match for your students and context.

## I Cannot Do Universal Design for Learning Because My District Uses a Curriculum with Scripted Lessons

UDL and scripted curriculum are not mutually exclusive. Scripted lessons are routinized and explicitly taught. Multiple ways of engaging the students, multiple ways of presenting the information, allowing multiple ways of expression, and multiple ways of assessment can be used during those highly structured routines. Even though the lesson may be written out for you, for example, you can read it to the students while they follow along with text and pictures on the interactive whiteboard. Even though the lesson lists the exact questions you must ask, students can answer verbally, sign, draw a picture, or write a sentence with their choice of writing materials while sitting in the seat of their choice.

## FORMAT OF THE BOOK

The book includes six sections: Section I: Overview, Section II: Strategies for Engagement, Section III: Strategies for Input, Section IV: Strategies for Output, Section V: Strategies for Assessment, and Section VI: A Living Resource. Sections II–IV parallel the principles of UDL as put forth by the National Center on Universal Design for Learning (2011), with some changes to fit the practical application purpose of this book. Rather than *means of representation* and *means of expression,* this book uses the terms *input* and *output.* This is an alternative way of thinking about each concept in daily practice by teachers. Section V presents strategies for the area of assessment. Assessment as its own category overlaps with output but goes further because it addresses multiple means of evaluating output. Varied strategies for input and output may be moot if teachers do not move beyond traditional, narrowly defined assessment methods. Last, Section VI provides many resources for future reference and a set of questions for teachers' reflection when adding new strategies.

### Strategy Pages

Each strategy page in Sections II–V follows the same user-friendly format. Tabs on the outside margin delineate the section name. Each strategy contains the following parts:

- *Top section:* This part provides a description of the strategy. Strategies will be provided for physical space, materials, classroom management, technology, content areas, executive functions, social skills, and transition to adulthood. There will be a blend of strategies for high-incidence and low-incidence learning needs, as well as a blend of physical-motor, social-emotional, cognitive, and linguistic strategies.

- *Try This:* This part provides a visual depiction of what the strategy looks like in practice, for example, a photo, a web site to visit for resources and materials, a story about how a teacher used the strategy in class, or another must-read book.

- *Why This Works:* This part lists five important concepts to consider when using a strategy: 1) the research base or existing literature about the idea, 2) opportunity for student involvement, 3) reasonable use by teachers, 4) maintaining high expectations for all students, and 5) equity and universality of implementation.

- *If...Then:* This part provides icons to show other sections in which the strategy would also fit if used in a slightly different way or for a slightly different purpose. For example, a word map would be a strategy for input if used by the teacher to impart new information and also a strategy for output if used by the student to show what he or she has learned.

## Strategies for You as You Read the Strategies

Here are some suggestions for reviewing each strategy and section:

- *Doodling or writing in the margins.* Creating a meaningful visual or jotting down a related quote are great ways to use the margins of the book to expand on ideas.

- *Sticky notes.* Sticky notes are a versatile way to take notes and organize information. They come in all shapes, colors, and sizes. Small sticky tabs can be used to indicate pages to return to, whereas larger ones can be used to elaborate on an idea. Color coding the notes distinguishes between ideas for different purposes or questions.

- *Voice notes.* Sometimes an idea is processed too quickly to write down the details before they are forgotten. In this case, some people find it more effective to make a voice recording. Digital tape recorders are relatively inexpensive and convenient in terms of size and intuitive use. Most smartphones have free apps for voice recordings.

- *Mind-mapping apps.* Most smartphones have several free apps for mind-mapping or creating webs of detailed concepts (see page 101 for this input strategy). The processes for creating the map may differ, but the premise is the same for all—a main concept is placed in the center, connected to details (Figure 1.2).

This book was designed to follow UDL principles—to be engaging, to be accessed in different ways, and to offer readers opportunities to develop and reflect on their own ideas.

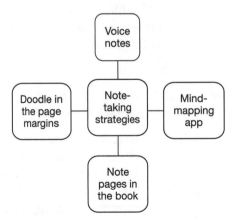

**Figure 1.2.** Strategies for reading this book.

# Strategies for Engagement…

# PROVIDING MULTIPLE MEANS OF ENGAGEMENT

UDL includes many different ways to engage students in learning. Each student is unique in his or her learning style, abilities, and ways of engaging in various learning opportunities. Some prefer working alone, whereas others prefer group work. Some prefer open-ended, highly subjective tasks, whereas others prefer structured, objective tasks. To increase engagement, teachers need to catch students' interest, as well as help them sustain effort and persist toward a goal, and self-regulate their learning behaviors (National Center on Universal Design for Learning, 2011).

To set the tone for effectively engaging students, it is important to decrease discomfort and distractions. Some students can focus their attention easily on a given task, whereas others have more difficulty filtering out distractions in the environment, some of which may cause discomfort or distress. There are many factors involved here to make sure the classroom is physically and emotionally comfortable. Physically, the temperature should be moderate, the lighting should be adequate, and the furniture should be appropriate for all students' needs. Emotionally, the classroom should be supportive, free of ridicule and judgment, and encouraging. Each student should be urged to take risks but not forced out of his or her comfort zone, which is unique to each student.

## Options for Catching Interest

One of the most effective ways to catch students' interests and encourage them to attend to important information is to provide choice and autonomy. Students can choose the process used to accomplish a task, the tools or materials used during the process, and the product they create to show their learning. Differentiated menus are an excellent example of offering choice to students. As long as the choices are appropriate—not too easy and not too challenging—providing choice increases interest and engagement.

Another important way to interest students is to offer relevant, valuable, authentic activities. Teaching them to work division problems in math for the purpose of completing a worksheet or test is not authentic. Bringing in a cake and teaching them to work a division problem so that each student receives an equal piece is relevant. Having students bring in real problems from home—How should the vegetable garden be divided? How can I double or halve a recipe? How much tile do I need to cover the bathroom floor?—and working out the problems to inform their families is valuable. Make sure activities are culturally relevant, as well as socially, developmentally, and individually appropriate.

## Options for Sustaining Effort and Persistence

Once the teacher has a student's interest, it is important to help the student persevere in his or her efforts. Sustaining effort on a task can be increased by frequently revisiting the goals and steps toward the goal so that the student can strive for the goal. Varying resources and changing materials can refresh engagement. Fostering collaboration and communication through carefully structured groups helps students guide each other toward task completion. Providing frequent feedback and showing the student how much progress has been made demonstrates how far he or she has come and how much is left to do.

## Options for Self-Regulation

For students to self-regulate their learning behaviors, they need to know what those behaviors are and how they can be improved. As a teacher, every time you find an effective strategy for a student, it is important that the student be made aware of the strategy and its positive effect. The more students know about their strengths, needs, and best strategies, the more they will be able to take charge of their own learning, including self-regulating their performance and progress. Areas in which a student should be self-aware include extrinsic (external) and intrinsic (internal) motivators, personal coping skills, self-assessment, and self-reflection. Some extrinsic motivators may be grades, prizes, or rewards (e.g., extra recess, computer time). Some intrinsic motivators may be pride in a job well done, excitement about the topic, or a feeling of being challenged. Coping skills that help students focus their attention or work through overwhelming situations include drawing or doodling, chewing gum, talking to a peer or counselor, and writing in a journal. Self-assessment and self-reflection are difficult to develop. It is not easy for people to step back, look at themselves objectively, and be honest and specific about how they are doing and how they can improve. Teachers can provide scaffolds that help students assess their own performance and reflect on ways to improve.

Fostering independence generally increases motivation and engagement. At any age, students are ready to take on a new task themselves. At 5 years old, it may be deciding which center to do first during independent work time. At 10 years old, it may be deciding which book to read for a book circle and developing discussion questions for the group. At 15 years old, it may be starting an extracurricular club and facilitating the meetings. The teacher's role is to scaffold and guide, not micromanage.

## CONSIDERATIONS

There are several considerations to keep in mind when thinking about how to engage diverse learners.

### Human Interests Are Unique and Dynamic

No two students are engaged the same way, even if they share commonalities. Not all students with autism, for example, are engaged in the same way, just as not all boys are engaged in the same way, and not all African American students are engaged the same way. Even identical twins have different perspectives and experiences that shape their unique interests. No two students are alike. Nor is any one student the same for very long. One thing this means for teachers is, essentially, that there is never a time for resting on your laurels. Once you have a great store of ways to catch your students' interests, you still need to keep looking for new ways to keep it fresh, novel, and age-appropriate. I do not have to tell you how quickly children grow and change.

### Sustained Effort, Persistence, and Self-Regulation Depend on Many Variables

Willis (2006) described the role of emotion and stress in students' abilities to process information, sustain attention, plan and set goals, problem-solve, critically analyze, and evaluate outcomes. In either a stressed or a bored state, the part of the brain's limbic system called the amygdala shifts into overdrive. In this state, information is channeled into fight-flight-freeze mode in which little higher order processing is possible. It is important to maintain a balance between stress and boredom. Students need to be challenged but not frustrated, and they need to feel comfortable in a predictable environment without being bored. Many things, both physical and emotional, can cause stress. Although teachers cannot predict, plan, or prevent some of them (e.g., coming down with a cold, not getting enough sleep, being excited or anxious about weekend plans, having a poor diet), we can be ready and make the classroom safe from other negative variables (e.g., fear of making a mistake in the classroom, lack of choice in assignment topics or peer partners, test anxiety, culturally irrelevant content).

## How It All Comes Together

Engagement is one of the principles of UDL, but it is also prominent in the other foundational theories of this book. Tomlinson and McTighe (2006) included it in the WHERETO Framework of Understanding by Design. The acronym stands for

- *What* to learn

- How to *Hook* and engage learners

- How to *Equip* students

- Encouraging learners to *Rethink* previous learning

- Promoting self-*Evaluation*

- *Tailoring* learning activities

- *Organizing* learning for maximum engagement and effectiveness

Two important points included here are the value of hooking students with introductory activities that "itch" the mind and draw them into learning, and immersing students in challenging tasks and problems at first, rather than making them climb the lower rungs of the ladder mastering basic concepts first. Tomlinson and McTighe (2006) found that tapping students' interests and allowing them choice of authentic tasks increased their learning productivity. Culturally responsive teaching theory includes choice and authenticity as important for engaging students, as is inductive, interactive, and communal problem solving (Gay, 2010).

Research on brain-based learning indicates that our brains are structured to better remember novel or unexpected events. These types of events put our brains on alert, better focused on what is to come next (Willis, 2006). Once the novelty has hooked them, students need opportunities to interact with the new information to sustain their attention.

Last, an essential part of believing in one's individuality—a main concept of full citizenship in the classroom—is understanding that each person has his or her own interests and personality. Discovering those individualized interests and incorporating them into new learning is critical in creating a classroom that engages everyone.

# Bulletin Board Borders

**Place bold, distinct borders around bulletin boards and wall displays.** Many teachers like to cover bulletin boards and classroom walls with displays of student work and decorations. This practice can help to create a shared space and to build classroom community. Sometimes, however, visual displays can be overwhelming to students who have difficulty processing a lot of visual stimuli. By placing a bold border that distinguishes the display from the background wall and from other displays, you can help students perceive each display as one piece instead of many pieces. In that way, the classroom can be engaging to all, while not overwhelming to some.

## Try This

Messy bulletin board

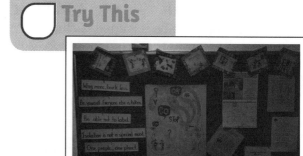

Bulletin board with border

## Why This Works

- **Research base.** It is based on neuropsychology research about figure–ground discrimination (National Center for Learning Disabilities, 2012).

- **Student involvement.** Students can evaluate displays for effectiveness, overstimulation, and engagement. Students can participate in creating displays and rotating work. Assigning someone to be the Bulletin Board Manager or Interior Decorator can be a classroom job.

- **Reasonable use.** It is simple, easy, and inexpensive for the teacher and/or students to implement.

- **Expectations maintained.** It makes the room more appealing yet not overstimulating. It does not lower expectations for knowledge or skill level for any student.

- **Equity and universality.** It recognizes diversity in the ways students are engaged and in the ways students process visual stimuli. All students can experience the visuals equitably without compromising the colorfulness or engaging quality of the classroom.

> → IF . . . THEN ←
>
> If the material on the bulletin board is used for instructional purposes, and the students learn more from the visually distinctive display, then this can also be a strategy for **Input.**
>
> INPUT
>
>

# Seating

**Offer varied seating.** An outdated belief is that in order to be engaged, a student must be sitting up straight in a chair, at a desk, with feet on the floor. Now we know that some students are more engaged when moving or standing. It is time to rethink seating in the classroom. Student desks and chairs may still work best for some, so they should continue to have their place—as long as they are adjustable—but more options need to be added. For example, using a stability ball instead of a standard chair turns a student desk into a newly engaging workspace. Bean bag chairs and yoga mats moved to quieter, more private areas of the classroom create a more relaxing space where some students are able to work longer and more efficiently. Small-group tables allow students to have company or collaborate in their work. Taller café tables allow students to stand and wiggle while engaged in tasks. In addition, seat cushions, supports, stools, and learning chairs are available.

## Try This

Stability balls

Bean bags

## Why This Works

- **Research base.** Comfortable, flexible seating in the classroom can increase engagement and motivation (Gargiulo & Metcalf, 2010).

- **Student involvement.** Students are able to explore and choose which furniture is most comfortable for them for various activities, which provides them opportunity to reflect on whether their level of engagement increases or decreases.

- **Reasonable use.** All of the seating variations mentioned are readily available. The cost may be considerable depending on the furniture.

- **Expectations maintained.** When the teacher believes that alternative seating can be used for learning and not just recreation, that belief is

Café table

passed to the students. Students are still expected to be engaged in the lesson and work and to use the furniture in a safe and respectful manner.

- **Equity and universality.** All seating variations must be available to everyone. Everyone in the classroom is entitled to a seat, so everyone should be entitled to a choice of seat.

➤ **IF . . . THEN** ◄

If stability balls, standing, and moving are used to benefit learning and behavior, as evidenced in multiple research studies (Kilbourne, 2009; Schilling, Washington, Billingsley, & Deitz, 2003; Shepard, 1997), then this can also be a strategy for **Input.**

INPUT

# Lighting

**Use different lighting.** Meeting the needs of all students in terms of lighting is difficult, especially if some students prefer bright lighting and others prefer dimmer or softer lighting. In the same open space, how do you provide both? There are classroom light filters commercially available. These fabric filters come in a variety of colors and are fastened over the bright ceiling lights in the classroom. Different colors can be used in different areas of the classroom to meet students' preferences and needs. Partitions also may help. Another solution is to turn off the overhead lighting altogether and use table and floor lamps with soft or full-spectrum light bulbs where needed or desired.

## Try This

Variable lighting

## Why This Works

- **Research base.** A summary of studies shows that good lighting contributes to the aesthetics of the learning space, as well as increased achievement and on-task behavior. In addition, colored filters can increase concentration and lessen visual fatigue (Engelbrecht, 2003; Jago & Tanner, 1999).

- **Student involvement.** Students can participate in the design of the classroom and placement of filters or lamps. Working in different areas of the room provides students with the opportunity to determine which lighting type and/or color is most effective for them.

- **Reasonable use.** Approved, heat-resistant light covers should be purchased and used only as instructed—it may not be safe to cover lights with any other fabric or cellophane. Any table or floor lamp will do as long as the lamps are stable and the cords are intact.

- **Expectations maintained.** Expectations of the students are not changed at all. The environment allows them to engage in and concentrate longer on the task at hand.

- **Equity and universality.** All lighting variations must be available to everyone to explore. More than one lighting type should be available at all times as student needs require.

> **→ IF . . . THEN ←**
>
> If the lighting and different color options in the visual environment are used to have an impact on perception of visual stimuli, then this can also be a strategy for **Input.**
>
> INPUT
>
>

# Fidget Toys

**Have a variety of fidget toys available.** Some students process auditory information more efficiently if simultaneously handling a small toy that keeps their hands busy. Collect many different kinds to appeal to many different sensory needs. Some ideas include small plush animals; hacky sacks; spiky rubber or squishy foam balls; one-piece wooden puzzles; toy metal cars with spinning wheels; sparkly liquid-filled tubes; beaded bracelets; or balloons filled with sand, rice, or flour. Fidget toys should be soothing, yet sturdy. Avoid toys that light up too brightly or make noise. Encourage students to try different kinds during different activities. Once you establish ground rules about safe and respectful use (e.g., no throwing, use a maximum of two toys at a time), it often takes little time for students to settle in to their favorite toy or even decide they do not need one at all. I have even found my college students stay engaged longer with their fidgets!

## Try This

Fidgets

## Why This Works

- **Research base.** Use of fidget toys enhances passive learning experiences, facilitates communication between both sides of the brain, and stimulates the release of chemicals vital to learning (Zawitz, 2009). Stalvey and Brasell (2006) also found that stress balls can provide the physical and sensory stimulation needed to focus attention.

- **Student involvement.** Students have choice of use, may contribute fidgets to the collection or make their own, and should help keep them clean and maintained.

- **Reasonable use.** Fidget toys are inexpensive, especially if homemade, and readily available at any retail store or online. Keeping a basketful in the classroom that is accessible to every student is simple.

- **Expectations maintained.** Students are expected to use the fidget toys safely and respectfully, as with any classroom materials. Fidget toys are used to engage in learning and work, not be excused from it.

- **Equity and universality.** A choice of fidgets are available to all students at all times.

> **► IF . . . THEN ◄**
>
> If the fidgets are used to enhance the processing of new information, then this can also be a strategy for **Input.**
>
> INPUT
>
>

# Professional Equipment

**Supply professional gear for student activities when possible.** Materials and equipment that are close to those used in the field by professionals bring a real-life feel to the task at hand. And they increase the feeling of significance, importance, and application of the knowledge and skills to future careers. For example, lab coats, nonprescription eyeglasses, folders and notebooks with company logos, ledgers, and forms in triplicate engage students as professionals in their work.

## Try This

Lab coat

## Why This Works

- **Research base.** Supplying professional materials when possible engages students by making the learning more meaningful and contextualized, which facilitates generalization of new knowledge to other settings (Rapp, 1997).

- **Student involvement.** Students can use the equipment and materials independently. They do not require any more preparation than typical supplies. Students should have the opportunity to reflect on the impact the materials has on their engagement.

- **Reasonable use.** These are inexpensive items that can be donated or found at thrift stores or garage sales. Triplicate paper that can be run through the printer to create custom forms is available from office supply stores.

- **Expectations maintained.** Students are achieving the same standards and mastering the same skills, but they are engaging with the tasks in a different way.

- **Equity and universality.** Connection to real-life situations is important for the learning styles and engagement of diverse learners. Being able to picture themselves in a particular role (e.g., scientist, business executive, teacher, historian) introduces every student to career choices.

→ IF . . . THEN ←

If professional equipment is used so that student learning is generalized and applied in other settings, then this can also be a strategy for **Output.**

OUTPUT

# Writing Surfaces

**Offer clever things to write on.** Familiar tasks in the classroom, such as practicing spelling words or solving math equations, can be more engaging if atypical or "retro" materials are used for writing out the answers. Clipboards, for example, can be used in any spot in the classroom, so writing can occur in fun places such as in bean bag chairs or in window seats rather than at a desk. There also is novelty in equipment that is hardly ever seen anymore, such as overhead projectors or label makers. An overhead projector placed in a learning center with transparencies and markers creates a new way to display work to peers in small groups. Punching out words or math products on a label maker can renew students' interest in a task.

 **Try This**

Label maker

Overhead projector

## Why This Works

- **Research base.** Classrooms that embrace UDL offer a variety of materials (both high-tech and low-tech) for presentation, engagement, and response (Gargiulo & Metcalf, 2010).

- **Student involvement.** Once these items are set up and students are instructed in their use, students can use any of these materials or pieces of equipment independently. Students can complete rating scales on how engaging an activity is when using each material. This data, coupled with level of performance, should be shared with students to show how the materials have an impact on their learning.

- **Reasonable use.** A clipboard for each student (so anyone can use one at any time) is reasonable because they are inexpensive. Label makers are more expensive (about $20–$40 at office supply stores), but only a few are needed for the whole class to share. An overhead projector could be taken out of storage, and only one is needed for the whole class. Chances are there is a supply room full of them!

- **Expectations maintained.** The spelling words, math problems, or writing prompts have not changed, just the materials with which the students can present their responses.

*(continued)*

- **Equity and universality.** If these writing surfaces are offered to everyone, students are welcome to explore and make choices about what is most engaging for them. Making the effort to supply various materials shows all students in the class that you want every subject area to be refreshing and interesting.

IF . . . THEN

If various tools are used so that students can better express themselves, then this can also be a strategy for **Output.**

OUTPUT

 Jobs

**Create authentic classroom jobs.** Job charts are ubiquitous in classrooms. To engage all students, classroom jobs should be more than just busy work. Titles for jobs should be the same as professional positions so that students can gain experience in areas of interest while feeling their efforts have a true impact on the classroom community. Rather than rotating small jobs to every student for a brief time, consider offering complex jobs needing many workers that are assigned for longer stretches so that students can develop higher level skills and solve problems relating to the work. Realistically not everyone in a community holds every job, but each person should do something to contribute to the community. Some people explore various jobs throughout their career, whereas others maintain one job over time.

## Why This Works

- **Research base.** Johnson and Thomas (2009) indicated that jobs that matter are part of caring classrooms that promote a sense of community, feelings of empowerment, and moral sensibility.

- **Student involvement.** Creating classroom jobs facilitates the highest level of student involvement. It makes it possible for teachers to step back and allow the students to completely run certain aspects of the classroom. Students can actively apply, interview, and evaluate their own and others' job performances.

### Try This

Christopher Simmons, a fifth-grade teacher, has students apply and interview for positions of Class Captain (takes care of morning attendance and lunch count and facilitates class meetings), Archivist (manages lesson materials and distributes handouts), Fire Chief (leads the line and takes attendance during a fire drill), Chairman of the Boards (cleans the whiteboards and sets up the SMART Board), Mail Carrier (delivers notes, paperwork to the office or other classrooms), Zookeeper (feeds class pets and cleans the habitats), Interior Designer (creates bulletin board displays), Librarian (manages the books and bins in the class library), Tech Specialist (turns on and off equipment as needed), Classroom Super (manages classroom clean-up), Gofer (fetches supplies or information from areas of the classroom or school), and Social Committee Members (plan parties and other events).

- **Reasonable use.** Training for the jobs will take more time at the beginning of the school year but will quickly diminish when students teach each other.

- **Expectations maintained.** Classroom jobs up the ante for students in terms of responsibility and self-management. In addition to academics, students are expected to maintain the physical classroom and contribute to the community, which is a lifelong skill.

*(continued)*

---

- **Equity and universality.** The authentic nature of the jobs, the choices provided, and the expectation that *all* students will contribute to the classroom sends the message that the classroom belongs to everyone and is the responsibility of everyone.

> **→ IF . . . THEN ←**
>
> If classroom jobs are used so that the teacher can determine level of independence and mastery on a daily or weekly basis while students practice and demonstrate job-related skills, then this can also be a strategy for **Assessment.**
>
> ASSESSMENT
>
>

# Meetings

**Hold regular class meetings.** Called many things—class meetings, morning meetings, class circles—and using many formats, these structured and regular times serve to engage students of all ages in their learning and classroom environment. Morning meetings, as outlined by Kriete (2002), consist of greeting, sharing, a group activity, and a morning message. The purposes of regular morning meetings are to set a tone of respect and trust that lasts throughout the day and beyond school walls; to address the needs to feel significant and to have fun; to repeat ordinary moments of respect so that students are able to interact in extraordinary ways; and to merge social, emotional, and intellectual learning.

Class meetings

Dr. Walter Cooper Academy (http://www.rcsdk12.org/10), a K–8 school built on the expeditionary learning model of engaging inquiry-based curriculum and development of positive school culture, starts every day with morning meeting time. Each classroom conducts its own meeting on most days, but on Wednesday mornings, the whole school gathers for a schoolwide meeting led by Principal Camaron Clyburn.

## Why This Works

- **Research base.** Kriete (2002); Nelson, Lott, and Glenn (2000); and Kohn (2006) described how class meetings develop a sense of belonging, empowerment, and capability in students. Class meetings provide students with decision-making opportunities so that they are more engaged and invested in the classroom community.

- **Student involvement.** The structure and routine of class meetings prepares students to eventually take over the meetings and facilitate them independently.

- **Reasonable use.** Class meetings are very simple, but their implementation is a process. Adhering to a predictable routine and scaffolding respectful interactions may take a few weeks or so depending on individual student needs.

- **Expectations maintained.** Class meetings uphold high expectations for students to collaboratively share, make decisions, plan, and reflect.

*(continued)*

- **Equity and universality.** Rapp and Arndt (2012) asserted that class meetings are one way to engage students by showing them they are welcome in the classroom. By allowing students to share responsibility for creating a safe and supportive environment, you show them that the classroom and its community belongs to everyone.

<table>
<tr><td>

→ IF . . . THEN ←

If the meetings are used to offer a responsive context for demonstrating social skills, then this can also be a strategy for **Output.**

OUTPUT

</td></tr>
</table>

# Smarty Pants

**Use Smarty Pants.** Liz Fyles, a first- and second-grade teacher, writes each student's name on a craft stick and places it in a pair of "Smarty Pants." Liz uses the plastic pants from Hasbro's Ants in the Pants game, but you can create them out of paper or fabric, or even use a pair of real pants with the legs sewn closed to create a bag of sorts. When students need a nudge to participate, or when you need to randomly choose a student for a task, you can choose one of your "Smarties" out of the pants. This is a cute, easy way to show each student that you believe he or she has smart things to contribute to the class. I have used this in college classes to encourage participation in discussion or assign students to small groups. Students can always pass, so choosing a Smarty is a fun, nonthreatening way to include every student.

**Try This**

Smarty pants

## Why This Works

- **Research base.** A series of studies stress that "students need a nurturing environment where they feel secure about learning, where the goal is success for every student and where students are confident they will receive mentoring and encouragement to prepare for their futures" (Southern Regional Educational Board, 2012, p. 1).

- **Student involvement.** The teacher opens the door for every student to participate. From there, the student has a choice as to whether or not he or she would like to contribute or participate.

- **Reasonable use.** Craft sticks are very inexpensive and available at any craft store. Writing each student's name on a stick is done quickly at the beginning of the year. The pants can be obtained or created very inexpensively as well.

- **Expectations maintained.** Students should be expected to contribute in some way. If they have difficulty initiating a contribution to large-group discussion or choosing their own partner or group, this is a way to scaffold them. The student should always be able to pass so that it does not feel threatening to be put on the spot, but if the student always passes, other ways should be used to evaluate his or her understanding, such as one-on-one sharing with the teacher or a buddy.

*(continued)*

- **Equity and universality.** This encourages every student and sends a message that everyone's thoughts, ideas, and participation are considered valuable.

→ IF ... THEN ←

If the Smarty Pants are used as an encouraging way for students to express their ideas during class discussion, then this can also be a strategy for **Output.**

OUTPUT

# Organized Classroom

**A place for everything, and everything in its place.** A big part of being responsive to students is classroom management—having a well-organized classroom in which the teacher and students alike can obtain materials they need easily, quickly, and independently. Items that are used most frequently should be plentiful, in view, and in reach, with no barriers. Bins and baskets are simple, neat, easily labeled receptacles for crayons, markers, papers, books, toys, math manipulatives, and equipment. Plenty of labeled hooks on the wall at heights accessible to every student ensure a place for everyone's things. A metal strip on the wall next to the door is a great place to stick hall and bathroom passes that have self-adhesive, magnetic tape (available at any craft store)

Organized shelves

on the back. Color-coded shelves and filing drawers keep books and papers in order. In addition, personal or individual items that are not meant for everyone's use, such as lunch boxes, clothing, eyeglasses, or assistive technology, should have a place to be stored safely and privately.

**Try This**

## Why This Works

- **Research base.** Classrooms that engage all students in a UDL philosophy allow students to find and return all materials, store personal items in individual spaces, and be safe at all times (Gargiulo & Metcalf, 2010).

- **Student involvement.** Even if storage is initially planned by the teacher, as the year progresses, students should be welcome to offer suggestions and changes. Involving the students in problem solving (e.g., "We decided to keep the counters in a sealed container so they do not spill, but not everyone can open the container. What suggestions do you have?") sends the message that it is everyone's right and everyone's responsibility to have a classroom that is fully accessible to all.

- **Reasonable use.** Though materials for organization (e.g., bins, baskets, hooks, clips, labels) are inexpensive and readily available, staying organized may be difficult for some. Getting help from a particularly organized colleague is easy to do, especially if you offer one of your talents in trade.

- **Expectations maintained.** Safe and respectful use of materials is maintained. In addition, students gain skills in caring for a shared space—doing their share, keeping others in mind, understanding how a classroom runs.

*(continued)*

- **Equity and universality.** If only the teacher can reach materials, is allowed to use them, or decides where they go, it is not everyone's classroom.

**IF . . . THEN**

If the classroom is organized so that all students can easily gain access to whatever they need to learn a new concept, then this can also be a strategy for **Input.**

INPUT

# ▪️◻️▪️ Interactive Whiteboards

**Utilize interactive whiteboards for lessons and class activities.** Interactive whiteboards such as SMART Boards encompass all three components of the UDL principle of engagement—catching students' interest, sustaining effort and persistence, and self-regulation. The possibilities for fun, engaging, high-quality lessons and activities using the board are practically endless.

Interactive whiteboard

Several web sites are available to provide ideas and prepared lessons or games:

- iSmartboard (http://www.ismartboard.com)

- PBS Kids Interactive Whiteboard Games (http://pbskids.org/whiteboard)

- Scholastic Interactive Whiteboard Lessons (http://www.scholastic.com/smarttech/teachers .htm)

- SMART Ideas for SMART Board Integration (http://abunday-smartboard.blogspot.com)

## Why This Works

- **Research base.** Smith and Pecore (2008) asserted that interactive whiteboards, because of their alignment with constructivist framework, allow for strong student autonomy and student-centered classroom environments, and interactive whiteboards bring more enthusiasm while learning.

- **Student involvement.** The key is to have the students interact with the interactive whiteboards as much as possible. Like any other tool, if only the teacher uses it, the level of engagement diminishes considerably.

- **Reasonable use.** Interactive whiteboards are costly but provide a significant bang per buck when used well. Portable interactive whiteboards that can be shared among classrooms are less expensive but have more issues with calibration because they are not stationary. Mini boards with interactive projections are another less-expensive option.

- **Expectations maintained.** Interactive whiteboards maintain achievement of all content area objectives plus collaboration skills! Students who have not yet developed writing skills often are highly motivated by demonstrating their success through tapping and dragging facilities (Somekh et al., 2007).

*(continued)*

- **Equity and universality.** As long as everyone can have access to the board, it is a tool that is inherently universal because it offers visual, auditory, and tactile experiences for an extremely wide range of abilities. As with other computer hardware, interactive whiteboards can be operated with a keyboard, fingers, a joystick, or a head switch. The boards have volume control, and all information can be captioned. The full-screen option removes distracting sidebars.

→ IF . . . THEN ←

If the interactive whiteboard activities are used to increase achievement in content areas for all students (as in Somekh et al. [2007], who explained that interactive white-boards as multimodal portals allow for the use of still images as well as moving images and sound to address the needs of students who have difficulty with text), then this can also be a strategy for **Input.**

INPUT

# Videoconferencing

**Use webcams and videoconferencing.** Having a guest speaker in class is an engaging change of pace for students, but scheduling an in-person visit is not always possible. With the technology of webcams and videoconferencing, more people are at our fingertips to have as guest speakers in class. Through such tools, teachers can connect with more than 50,000 teachers worldwide for collaborative problem solving. Students can register for a group talk with a journalist and world hunger activist, for example, hear book authors read their works live, interview Olympic athletes, practice musical instruments with others, chat with peers around the globe, and more!

**Try This**

Videoconferencing

## Why This Works

- **Research base.** Ellis (2009) indicated that the social interaction through videoconferencing allows students to reflect and reconsider, get support, and engage in authentic problem solving.

- **Student involvement.** Additional benefits outlined by Ellis (2009) include improved learning strategies, perseverance, and self-reliance. Students can reflect on ways to enhance their own learning and become independent through the use of videoconferencing.

- **Reasonable use.** Hardware needs include a webcam. Many new computers have them built in; otherwise, external accessories can be purchased. Videoconferencing software is free and can be downloaded over the Internet. A relatively fast Internet connection is needed.

- **Expectations maintained.** Videoconferencing can be used to enhance instruction in any content area. Students are also expected to use the Internet safely and professionally.

- **Equity and universality.** Any accommodations needed for computer use (e.g., adapted equipment, closed captioning) are used when videoconferencing.

**→ IF . . . THEN ◄**

If videoconferencing is used to enhance instruction, then this can also be a strategy for **Input.**

INPUT

⊕

# Blogs

**Create blogs.** Students can learn a lot from each other during class discussions. Some students, however, are more able or willing to contribute their thoughts in a large-group setting. Sometimes, there is just not enough time to hear from everyone. Blogs are a way technology can help to expand the discussion beyond the confines of classroom walls and time. During other parts of the day or outside of school, students can access the blog through the classroom web site and add their thoughts without the pressure of time or a face-to-face audience.

Shawn Ranney, a fourth-grade teacher, creates content-specific blogs on his classroom web site and posts questions that all students can access and respond to.

## Try This

Blogs

For the "Reading…Does the Body Good" blog, Mr. Ranney posts a question for each book the students has read for class. For example, the question posted for *Number the Stars,* a book in which the lives of the characters are affected by the injustices of war, is "What injustices do you see in the world today that might provoke you to exercise courage?"

For the "Science…Rules!" blog, Mr. Ranney posts a scenario in which a student needs help to solve a scientific problem. One example is Adam's need to remove a heavy tree stump in order to put in a frog pond. The blog encourages the students to use their knowledge of simple machines to help Adam figure out how to move the tree stump.

## Why This Works

- **Research base (teacher recommendation).** As Mr. Ranney reports, "This medium is highly engaging for all students, and it encourages more participation in a more open-ended format. Students not only share their own thoughts, but eagerly comment on each other's."

- **Student involvement.** Students have the opportunity to engage with the content in two important ways—they post their individual thoughts *and* construct a communal response by introducing new things for their classmates to think about with each blog response.

- **Reasonable use.** This is extremely simple to create once you are familiar with the web-posting process. It takes only a moment to post a question, but it may take several minutes a day to read through students' responses. The teacher only needs to jump in to clarify any misconceptions or acknowledge the thread of ideas.

- **Expectations maintained.** Blogging holds students accountable for accurate and relevant knowledge and skills around a particular topic. It also holds them accountable for appropriate use of public forums on the Internet.

- **Equity and universality.** In the classroom, if all students have access to the computer equipment, they have equitable access to the blogs. At home, computer equipment and Internet access may vary. Class time, study halls, and before/after school hours should be free for students to use school computers to blog. Preference can be given to those who do not have access at home.

→ IF . . . THEN ←

If the blogs are used to provide another venue for students to express their knowledge on a particular topic or issue, then this can also be a strategy for **Output.**

OUTPUT

# Tactile Activities

**Offer tactile practice.** When we think of reinforcing skills through more than one modality, we often think of auditory and visual means. Tactile activities, however, are seldom engaged. Tracing letters, spelling words, solving math problems, or drawing a picture in different materials (e.g., shaving cream, sand, rice, glue, finger paint, modeling clay) provides the brain with another way to learn. It is novel and stimulating—oh, and fun!

## Try This

Group activities

Rice

## Why This Works

- **Research base.** Willis (2006) explained that learning skills in more than one way—through more than one of the senses—increases neural pathways in the brain, making it easier for the information to be stored, used, and connected to other learning.

- **Student involvement.** Students can come up with ideas for different things to use. Trying them once or twice and having the students reflect on their use will help them decide if the mess and cleanup is worth it, or if it is feasible given the needs in the class. Peanut butter, for example, is a great new idea, but it is difficult to clean up and may be dangerous if anyone has a nut allergy.

- **Reasonable use.** Many items are very reasonably priced and readily available at a dollar store. Many of them are reusable (e.g., rice, beans, sand, clay).

- **Expectations maintained.** Using tactile materials means academic skills and cleanup skills are practiced!

Shaving cream

- **Equity and universality.** Choice, of course, is important because some textures may be offensive to students with sensitive sensory needs. Writing in tactile materials on the desktop offers a way for students to create text even if they have difficulty grasping a pen or pencil.

Letters

**IF . . . THEN**

If tactile activities are used to provide students with a different way to create a response, then this can also be a strategy for **Output.**

OUTPUT

# Bag of Writing Ideas

**Have students fill a bag with items to prompt writing ideas.** Some students struggle when it comes to thinking of a topic for creative writing. To support this process and make the writing experience more meaningful for your students, start out the school year by having them fill a paper lunch bag with small items at home that remind them of things they love, fun experiences, or interesting hobbies. They can keep the bags in their desks or in a writing center in the classroom. When they are prompted to write and find themselves stuck for a topic, encourage them to look through the items in their idea bags. The personal connection to the object often triggers a story to tell.

Bag of writing ideas

## Why This Works

- **Research base.** Effective prompts are those that have a personal connection for the writer, allow for choice, and allow the writer to draw on experiences (Education Northwest, 2013).

- **Student involvement.** Students are involved in this strategy from beginning to end. They collect their own prompts to fill their bag, they decide which ones they will write about and in which order, and they are the experts on their own writing topics.

- **Reasonable use.** All you have to provide is a bag for the students to use.

- **Expectations maintained.** Students become more independent in the writing process because they do not rely on the teacher for a topic and are their own expert on the items in the bag.

- **Equity and universality.** This strategy is culturally responsive and is used to prompt creative expression regardless of supports used in the writing process.

> ▶ IF . . . THEN ◀
>
> If bags of writing ideas are used to provide a personal connection to writing assignments that helps students get started in expressing thoughts in writing, then this can also be a strategy for **Output.**
>
> OUTPUT
>
>

#  Mnemonics

**Use mnemonics to facilitate memory of learned information.** Mnemonics are techniques that help students recall factual information that has been learned. Once a student understands a concept, mnemonics can help the student remember the details or factual information related to the concept so that the student does not have to rely on the teacher, notes, or other external factors to remember everything. Recall is facilitated by making connections to familiar words, letters, images, or ideas. Mnemonics can be used for any subject area and can be verbal, physical, or written. Effective mnemonics use multiple senses, have emotional connections, use humor or pleasant or vivid images, and contain symbols or pictures.

 **Try This**

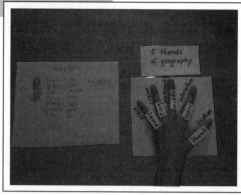

Mnemonics

## Why This Works

- **Research base.** Providing multiple means of engagement includes providing options for self-regulation (CAST, 2011). Mnemonics (or mnemonic devices) are one way students can regulate their own learning by triggering their recall of important information.

- **Student involvement.** Students should be encouraged to make up their own mnemonics because they are more effective if they have a personal connection.

- **Reasonable use.** Mnemonics are easy to create with students. You can make posters or simply write them down on a piece of paper.

- **Expectations maintained.** The facts recalled using mnemonics are not a substitute for the understanding of the concepts behind them or the application of the information.

- **Equity and universality.** Mnemonics create responsive ways for students to make connections to and obtain access to new learning.

> **→ IF . . . THEN ←**
>
> If mnemonics are used to help students recall information so that they can express new learning and elaborate on ideas with details, then this can also be a strategy for **Output.**
>
> OUTPUT
>
>

---

# Computer Software Programs

**Use software programs.** Countless skills can be reinforced through the use of computer software. Being on the computer, playing video games, or creating images and texts engages students in a different—digital—medium for working on skills. Computer programs offer tools for text-to-speech, speech-to-text, supported reading and writing, math, collaboration, and study skills. There are many great programs.

## Why This Works

- **Research base.** Software that goes beyond seductive bells and whistles and engages students in learning skills provides students with challenges, adjustable scaffolds, feedback on performance, and options (CAST, 2012).

- **Student involvement.** Students are able to be independent with the software programs. Most have tutorials and performance feedback built in.

- **Reasonable use.** Some programs can be downloaded for free. Others are available for individual users or for schoolwide use.

- **Expectations maintained.** Students should not be placed in front of the computer as a replacement for instruction. However, as a supplement, this is a valuable tool for holding students accountable for skill development and responsible computer use.

- **Equity and universality.** Supports are included in the programs. Adapted hardware makes it accessible to all.

## Try This

Here is a list of web sites to get you started:

**CAST Learning Tools**
http://www.cast.org/learningtools/index.html

**Ed Tech Solutions**
http://teachingeverystudent.blogspot.com/2007/06/free-technology-toolkit-for-udl-in-all.html

**Thinking Reader by Tom Snyder Productions**
http://www.tomsnyder.com/products/product.asp?sku=THITHI

**UDL Strategies**
https://udlstrategies.wikispaces.com/Multiple+Means+of+Engagement

**VizZle Visual Learning**
http://www.monarchteachtech.com/vizzle

→ IF . . . THEN ←

If software games and activities are used so that new skills are learned and reinforced, then this can also be a strategy for **Input.**

INPUT

# Games

**Collect board and card games.** What's more engaging than a board game or card game—especially if there are many to choose from? Playing a game is an excellent way to reinforce many academic and social skills, but it does not feel like skill practice. There are several adapted games and game pieces to meet various physical, sensory, or cognitive needs, for example, large foam dice or dice with raised markers and numerals printed on each side, checker and chess pieces with pegs on the bottom that fit easily into holes on the board, and magnetic boards so pieces stay put.

**Try This**

Games

## Why This Works

- **Research base.** Games are a fun and effective way to build skills, such as negotiating, taking turns, following rules, being a gracious winner or loser, sharing, patience, and strategizing (Lavoie, 2005a).

- **Student involvement.** Students are responsible for set up, cleanup, and maintenance of the games. Self-reflection sheets included in each game box can be completed individually or collaboratively by the players. Questions on the sheet might be, "Was playing this game a good use of your time for practicing _____?" or "How could you modify the rules of the game in order to practice ____?"

- **Reasonable use.** Games are relatively inexpensive, ranging from $5 to $20, or they can be found at garage sales for considerably less. Only one of each game is typically needed for the whole classroom to share, although having multiple decks of cards is a good idea. A few new games each year builds an impressive classroom library of engaging teaching tools. One classroom planned a game drive that outfitted several rooms with many gently used or new games.

- **Expectations maintained.** If you walked by a classroom full of students playing board or card games, you might assume it was free time. However, very effective academic and social skill learning is truly taking place!

- **Equity and universality.** The teacher's job is to offer choice in games and grouping while making careful note as to which students consistently choose or avoid a certain activity. One way to encourage students to move outside of their comfort zone on occasion is to set up carefully planned game stations and have small groups rotate through. All of the games should be accessible to everyone.

> **▶ IF . . . THEN ◀**
>
> If games are used so that the teacher can observe and gather a great deal of formative evaluation information, then this could also be a strategy for **Assessment.**
>
> ASSESSMENT
>
>

---

# Grouping

**Use various grouping.** Changing up the grouping for classroom lessons or activities provides everyone with their most engaging situation. It is important for everyone to have practice at times working alone, in pairs, in small groups, and in large groups, but students should have times when they can choose, too. For the times when the teacher selects the group size, having prearranged groups will save a lot of transition time. At the beginning of each marking period, write each student's name on an index card. Create groups by labeling the cards with symbols (e.g., numbers, letters, stickers, words) so that each student is grouped with different classmates in various group sizes. Now all you need to say is "number groups" or "animal groups" depending on the size group that is most appropriate.

Gouping cards

## Why This Works

- **Research base.** Cooperative learning in the classroom has positive effects on academic achievement, relationships, the development of English proficiency, acceptance of diverse students, self-esteem, liking of self and others, and attitudes toward school and teachers (Success for All, 2012). In addition, research shows that independent learning can increase student motivation, academic achievement, and self-regulatory skills (Meyer, Haywood, Sachdev, & Faraday, 2008), indicating that various grouping is important.

- **Student involvement.** Once students have been in each grouping situation and have been given ample opportunity to select their own arrangements, they should be involved in reflecting on appropriate group sizes for various activities and reflecting on the arrangements they find most or least helpful.

- **Reasonable use.** The only resource needed is time. It takes some time initially to create grouping cards, and it takes a few minutes to have students choose or form groups.

- **Expectations maintained.** When students are in groups larger than two, it is important to carefully assess the performance of each group and to scaffold accountability by all group members.

- **Equity and universality.** As long as students are sometimes provided with choice in group size and members, as well as an opportunity to reflect on the effectiveness, this is a responsive strategy that promotes citizenship and inclusion in the classroom.

→ IF . . . THEN ←

If small groups are used so that students can cooperatively formulate and present their work and responses, then this can also be a strategy for **Output.**

OUTPUT

#  Dice

**Use dice to engage students in cooperative review of lessons.** Dice can be used in a number of ways to bring students together in a cooperative group to review lessons in any content area. By using dice as is, adding your own stickers, or even purchasing blank dice that students can write on (see Super Duper Publications at http://www.superduperinc.com), you can create several review activities for multiplication facts, vocabulary or spelling words, historic dates, or scientific symbols. Each student in the group can roll a die or one person can roll while others answer. More students mean more ideas and more ways to review content.

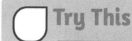 **Try This**

Dice

##  Why This Works

- **Research base.** Sharp (2012) summarized research indicating that games, when used as supplemental activities, are engaging and motivating, leading students to persevere with a task.

- **Student involvement.** Students can engage in this activity independently from the teacher. They can make up their own variations and determine whether they want the activity to be competitive or not. Students can also create their own labels for the dice.

- **Reasonable use.** This activity takes as much time to set up as does creating a worksheet for homework. A pack of six dice can be purchased at most dollar stores. Super Duper Publications offers a pack of six blank dice with 1,000 labels for $9.95.

- **Expectations maintained.** The students are learning the same content taught in lessons. The dice offer a new, engaging way for them to practice together with many different examples and answers.

- **Equity and universality.** Because the labels on the dice can be changed, they can be created to fit the needs of any student. Adaptive dice rollers are devices that roll dice by pressing a switch.

> ➤ IF . . . THEN ◄
>
> If dice are used so that students can evaluate themselves and each other on the answers to the questions created from rolling the dice, then this can also be a strategy for **Assessment.**
>
> ASSESSMENT

# Redefine Bullying

**Redefine bullying.** This is a different kind of strategy. It means changing an understanding of a fundamental concept in the classroom and school. The way bullying is typically conceptualized, there is a bully and a victim, and sometimes a bystander. This implies that there are "good guys" and "bad guys," which erodes the community that is essential to creating an inclusive environment in which everyone belongs and everyone is valued. Schools and classrooms that have zero-tolerance and no-questions-asked policies toward bullying and standardized punishments for bullies are failing to support the needs of all students. There is nothing cut and dry or easily defined about bullying. When one student is aggressive in some way toward another, all of the students have needs that should be met and skills to be learned. Bullying should be redefined as conflicts that need to be collaboratively solved. The focus of the classroom should be redefined toward recognizing everyone's strengths while supporting everyone's weaknesses. If we do this, we stop sending the message that there are good guys and bad guys, and we start sending the message that we are all in it together to help each other solve problems.

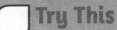

**Try This**

**Must-reads**

Cowhey, M. (2006). *Black ants and Buddhists: Thinking critically and teaching differently in the primary grades.* Portland, ME: Stenhouse Publishers.

Sapon-Shevin, M. (2007). *Widening the circle: The power of inclusive classrooms.* Boston, MA: Beacon Press.

Sapon-Shevin, M. (2010). *Because we can change the world: A practical guide to building cooperative, inclusive classroom communities* (2nd ed.). Boston, MA: Allyn & Bacon.

## Why This Works

- **Research base.** Kliewer's (1998) concept of a shared social place is that of a place where each individual is valued and where each individual can make mistakes without fear of failure or persecution.

- **Student involvement.** Every student is involved in a shared social place. Each student is accountable for him- or herself and for helping to support others. Students should be guided through opportunities to address issues and reflect on possible solutions.

- **Reasonable use.** This is difficult not because of cost or availability of resources. This is difficult because it entails a paradigm shift and patience as a community of interdependence and respect is established over time in the classroom.

- **Expectations maintained.** Redefining bullying does not mean that aggressive behavior is okay or will be tolerated. It still means that behavior must stop immediately. Redefining bullying means that the student who engages in aggressive behavior will not be labeled a bully or punished and condemned as a bad person in the community. That student will be valued and supported in learning new skills. Everyone will be expected to work with everyone, not just the ones who are easiest to work with.

- **Equity and universality.** This is bottom line acceptance of everyone as a valued member of the community. This is accepting without "excepting." The inclusive classroom is for everyone, no exceptions.

**→ IF . . . THEN ←**

If the redefinition of bullying is used to provide a framework for expressing needs and coming up with solutions, then this can also be a strategy for **Output.**

OUTPUT

# Using the Arts

**Use the arts to develop executive functions.**
The challenge to all teachers is to make the content they are teaching compelling—to fight off boredom and frustration that can lead to disengagement and inappropriate behavior. Thinking outside of the box to incorporate art, music, and drama into lessons does not have to be elaborate or time consuming. Several simple ideas can grab students' attention, awaken their curiosity, and stave off boredom and frustration:

- Dress in costume, use props, and/or use different voices for different characters in the lesson's reading.

- Play a song at the beginning of the lesson. There are several short, very catchy tunes by Schoolhouse Rock and They Might Be Giants.

- Show a strange object to introduce a new concept. When I teach about assistive technology in my introductory inclusive education courses, the students play "What am I?" with hard-to-identify, customized items. My students consistently list it as one of the most engaging activities.

- Show compelling photographs, or reveal pieces of a covered photograph over time until students can identify it.

- Show video clips.

## Try This

Using the arts

## Why This Works

- **Research base.** Willis (2012) explained that all new information enters the brain through sensory input, but there is a filter that allows only about 1% of that input in each second. This filter, called the reticular activating system, favors novel, unusual, curiosity-piquing stimuli (e.g., art, music, voices, strange objects) when deciding which information will pass through to the higher-thinking prefrontal cortex to strengthen the executive functions.

- **Student involvement.** Students can bring in objects, costumes, or photos that connect with units of study. This provides a personal connection that is likely to sustain their attention and engagement over a longer period of time.

- **Reasonable use.** As you build your collection, it is quick and simple to incorporate something novel into the anticipatory set of your lessons.

- **Expectations maintained.** When students are engaged for longer periods of time, the expectations for learning details and exploring new avenues of thought may actually be raised.

- **Equity and universality.** There is no one right way to connect with a lesson. Incorporating visual arts, music, and drama appeals to each student's experiences, culture, and background knowledge in a unique way.

→ IF . . . THEN ←

If arts are used to reduce stress so that the brain can more effectively and efficiently process new learning, then this can also be a strategy for **Input.**

INPUT

# Cue Signals

**Customize cue signals.** Some students have internal mechanisms that remind them when to make a transition, take a break, ask for help, keep an eye on the time, or follow the steps in a classroom procedure. Some do not, and they need external reminders. Some cues can be posted around the room that apply to all students—the day's agenda; what to do when work is finished; reminders to cleanup materials, homework, and mail bins. Other cues can be taped to each student's desk, customized to individual needs—a reminder to wear glasses, a checklist of tasks to accomplish in a particular order, behavioral goals. The cues can be in text or list form, include a series of individual icons or pictures, be on a storyboard, or be given by hand or sound signals. Instead of just a written reminder at the craft center (e.g., "Remember to clean up!"), add a photo of the center when it is tidy and organized. For individualized cues, the student may choose a symbol that is particularly meaningful, such as a picture of an eagle flying over a clock tower as a reminder to keep an eye on the time.

## Try This

Cues

## Why This Works

- **Research base.** Golden (2012) spoke to the importance of visual communication support for functional routines in the classroom, as well as behavioral expectations, time management, and material management.

- **Student involvement.** Students should be involved in suggesting ideas for classroom cue signals and should have the opportunity to share their individualized cues and reflect on why it is important to have those reminders. For example, when the teacher mentions that names are often left off of papers, a class meeting about effective reminders will generate several collaborative ideas that are meaningful and relevant to the students.

- **Reasonable use.** Cues are easy to create by hand or computer. The only cost may be in laminating cue cards.

- **Expectations maintained.** Students are still expected to independently perform skills and gain knowledge. It is important to separate the reminder from the skill. The cue removes the reminding from another person and provides an external support that the student can use in the future.

- **Equity and universality.** The benefits of cues have a ripple effect. There may be one or two students who rely on them heavily, but everyone in the class benefits to some degree. In one classroom, a visual reminder about the morning arrival routine was posted near one student's cubby so that she could become more independent in getting ready for the day. Other students benefited from the visual because it relieved their anxiety about the rushed morning as they focused on arrival one step at a time. Still other students benefited because it reminded them to turn in their homework. Everyone in the class can benefit from cues because students are learning that they are all different and supported in different ways toward success.

→ IF . . . THEN ←

If cue signals are used to provide a support for students to express their abilities independently, then this can also be a strategy for **Output.**

OUTPUT

# Minecraft Video Game

**Check out Minecraft—a planning, goal-setting video game.** Minecraft is a video game for PC and Mac formats, as well as other platforms. It has two modes. Creative mode allows players to build constructions out of textured cubes in a 3D procedurally generated world, with no threat of darkness or enemy. Survival mode requires players to acquire resources before they can build, while also warding off monsters at night. This video game enhances focus, as effort is needed to get started and then maintain attention to tasks; flexibility, as the player adapts and adjusts to changing conditions; organizational skills, as the player arranges and coordinates materials and activities in order to complete a task; and planning, as the player develops a systematic approach for setting and achieving goals.

Minecraft

## Why This Works

- **Research base (teacher recommendation).** If you plug the phrase "Minecraft as a teaching tool" into any search engine, you will discover dozens of ways in which teachers are incorporating the video game into lessons in every content area with great results.

- **Student involvement.** Individual group activities can be developed in which students discuss the results of their efforts.

- **Reasonable use.** The app for a smartphone or tablet typically costs under $10. The software for a computer is typically under $30.

- **Expectations maintained.** The benefits of this video game are in the hands of the user. As with interactive whiteboards or other instructional technology, simply purchasing the tool does not transform teaching and learning. Imaginative, engaging, planful use of the tool is essential.

- **Equity and universality.** As with blogging, playing the video game depends on computer access. In the classroom, if all students have access to the computer equipment, they have equitable access to the game. At home, computer availability and use will vary. Class time, study halls, and before/after school hours should be free for students to use school computers. Preference can be given to those who do not have access at home.

> **→ IF . . . THEN ←**
>
> If Minecraft is used as a different way for students to perform planning and organizational skills, then this can also be a strategy for **Output.**
>
> OUTPUT
>
>

# Bingo

**Use bingo to build a set of transition skills.** The list of skills to master for independent adult living can be overwhelming. By displaying the skills needed in a novel format and encouraging the student to decide the order in which to work on them, the student is more engaged, empowered, and autonomous in the process. A bingo (lotto) board lends itself to organizing a long list into subsets. The boards can be made with more or fewer squares. A board might contain several different goals, or it might contain several components in one goal. The bingo board is then used as a record of progress. Over days or weeks, as the student acquires each skill, the teacher and student together record notes in each box or attach work samples, photos, and so forth that demonstrate the accomplishment.

**Try This**

Transition bingo

## Why This Works

- **Research base.** This transition-to-adulthood bingo board is a modified version of an anchor activity suggested by Tomlinson (2003). Activities such as these provide students with productive choices.

- **Student involvement.** Students are fully involved in the completion of the tasks. They can decide where to start and at which pace to work toward completion of the whole board. They can be involved in placing the tasks or goals on the board and recording their progress.

- **Reasonable use.** The goals and tasks are set for the student as part of the transition process. This strategy simply entails applying them to a more engaging format.

- **Expectations maintained.** This strategy maintains the goals for students and expects them to make decisions about the progress they make.

- **Equity and universality.** Transition plans for students are highly individualized, but the format can be used for anyone's goals.

> → IF . . . THEN ←
>
> If transition bingo is used so that teachers can evaluate students on their progress toward each goal, then this can also be a strategy for **Assessment.**
>
> ASSESSMENT
>
>

# Real-Life Situations

**Provide experience with real-life situations.**
As teachers, there are many skills we teach by talking about examples or role playing the application. Instead of pretending and talking the students through, we need to create an actual opportunity to use the skill and reflect. We often hear ourselves telling students that they are learning a particular concept or skill because it will help them in the real world. What we need to remember is that school is the real world. There are plenty of situations in school in which students can use real-world skills, for example, discussing a frustration with a teacher or administrator, asking for additional supports or reevaluation of a piece of work, or applying for a position in a club. Rather than talk about the future when skills may come in handy, establish school situations to be like out-of-school situations.

 **Try This**

**Must-read**

Thoma, C.A., Bartholomew, C.C., & Scott, L.A. (2009). *Universal design for transition: A roadmap for planning and instruction.* Baltimore, MD: Paul H. Brookes Publishing Co.

Real-life situations

## Why This Works

- **Research base.** Tomlinson and McTighe (2006) summarized that tapping students' interests and allowing them choice of authentic tasks increased their learning productivity. Culturally responsive teaching theory includes choice and authenticity as important for engaging students, as is inductive, interactive, and communal problem solving (Gay, 2010).

- **Student involvement.** Students' needs and interests drive this strategy. Assigning tasks to be learned in real-life situations will not motivate them the same way as following their lead. When a student indicates a goal to be achieved or a skill to be learned, seek out authentic real-life ways for that to happen.

- **Reasonable use.** This is a schoolwide endeavor. Creating processes in the school that are true to adult life processes takes time and effort collaborating with colleagues.

- **Expectations maintained.** This ups the ante for many skills a student acquires. Completing an application and a year-end performance review with a club advisor builds more skills than simply showing up for a club meeting, for example.

- **Equity and universality.** With supports in place, all students benefit from authentic experiences. The supports should be authentic as well, matching what the students will use once they graduate from high school. Using a smartphone to take a photo of the assignment board in class is real-life authentic. Relying on the teacher or a friend to write down the assignments for you is not.

→ IF . . . THEN ←

If real-life situations are used so that the teacher can determine if students apply knowledge and skills appropriately in an authentic context, then this can also be a strategy for **Assessment.**

ASSESSMENT

# Invite People to Meetings

**Invite trusted individuals to meetings.** Cassie Pruitt, a high school teacher, suggested that students attend the annual meetings to plan their IEPs. In addition, as students reach high school and these meetings include person-centered planning for the transition to adult life, she encourages them to invite trusted individual(s) who will be part of their lives beyond high school. Beyond a parent, this might be a sibling, friend, mentor, neighbor, or counselor. The trusted individual can help plan supports for adult life that are truly by, for, and with the student, making it a life-planning meeting rather than a school-planning meeting. In addition, the student can create and talk through a PowerPoint presentation that follows the entire IEP process from assessing current levels of performance, to setting goals, to listing supports and services in each area of adult life.

Invitations to meetings

## Why This Works

- **Research base.** Thoma, Bartholomew, and Scott (2009) asserted that students are best prepared for adulthood when they leave high school with a plan for their lives in many areas, such as higher education, community living, housing, employment, and recreation.

- **Student involvement.** The student is not an attendee of this meeting but is a facilitator and a host. Everyone's contributions help guide the meeting, but it should be chaired by the student.

- **Reasonable use.** The most difficult part is scheduling a time for many people to meet.

- **Expectations maintained.** The IEP and transition plan create a structure and template for the meeting. Talking through each of the sections ensures that all areas are covered.

- **Equity and universality.** Everyone has the right to steer his or her own future, regardless of how extensive the supports need to be.

→ IF . . . THEN ←

If invitations to meetings are used so that teachers can evaluate the appropriate use and application of invitations and hosting a guest speaker, then this can also be a strategy for **Assessment**.

ASSESSMENT

# Strategies for Input...

# PROVIDING MULTIPLE MEANS OF INPUT

You have planned and created multiple ways to engage students. You have caught their interest, sustained their effort, and provided ways for them to self-regulate. Now it is time to consider the second principle of UDL. You must provide multiple means of representation—multiple ways to "input" content to be learned.

No matter how engaged your students are, if you just provide the content in one way, only the students who can obtain access to it that way are going to benefit from it. If you present it in multiple ways, three things happen: 1) more students are going to have access to the new learning, 2) the new information will be reinforced in multiple ways, and 3) students will be more likely to become expert learners because they will be familiar with multiple ways to receive information and thus will know what works best for them and can explore a range of ways to learn new information.

To input the new learning, students need to be able to 1) perceive the information; 2) understand language, mathematical expressions, and symbols; and 3) comprehend or assign meaning to the information.

## Options for Perception

To understand what it means to perceive new learning, we need to make a distinction between sensing and perceiving. Often, senses are confused with perceptions. The senses (i.e., sight, hearing, smell, taste, touch) allow us to detect or sense environmental stimuli. Perception is what allows us to understand or bring meaning to the stimuli once we have sensed it. So, it is possible to sense something but not be able to perceive it. It is also possible for two different people to sense the exact same stimuli but perceive it in different ways, as in the case of optical illusions. When a teacher presents new information to students in a visual format, a student might see it but not be able to bring meaning to it (i.e., perceive it) or the student might bring meaning to it in a different way than another student might.

## Options for Understanding Language, Mathematical Expressions, and Symbols

Written information is not only represented in letters and words but is also represented in numbers and symbols. Not everyone understands these lexicons the same way. Some people are more comfortable with words, whereas others are more adept at understanding numbers and mathematical symbols. Some have difficulty with both. This depends on the individual's processing style, cultural background, language, and lexical knowledge (National Center on Universal Design for Learning, 2011).

There are several ways to make written information more accessible to all students. Vocabulary, numbers, and symbols should be paired with alternative representations of their meaning—photos, illustrations, graphs, charts, or physical models. Not everyone will choose the same representation. A curriculum that is universally designed for learning will use various representations for all information.

All jargon, slang, and idiomatic expressions should be translated and explained. Structural rules and relationships should be made more explicit, such as the syntax in a sentence or the properties in equations. Make sure everything is available in the student's first language, including ASL for those who sign. This last suggestion is particularly important because students who are learning English as a second language enter classrooms and need access to content presented in their first language.

## Options for Comprehension

Comprehension occurs when a student takes new information and translates it into useable knowledge. This is an active process that includes attention to select bits of information, integrating new information with existing knowledge, and categorizing the integrated information (Nelson, 2014).

It is no surprise that comprehension can be improved when teachers use many different ways to activate existing knowledge. The more connections you can make from what students already know to new information that is learned, the more opportunities you open for students to comprehend it. The key to comprehension is to connect, connect, connect. Anchor new knowledge to what the students already know. Ask them about their experiences, and have them share those experiences with the whole class. Use metaphors and analogies to illustrate concepts. These can also be very powerful in helping students understand how they learn so that they can be their own best advocates, a characteristic of expert learners.

It is also very important—maybe most important—to teach students *how* they best make connections in order to perceive and comprehend different types of new information. Some students are able to make conclusions on their own about their learning preferences and abilities. Others need to be shown and taught. Talking through reflective questions should happen often: "I notice you draw when you listen to a lesson. What do you think about when you draw? Does it help you stay focused on my voice, or do you stop hearing my voice? What do you draw? Do you draw what you are hearing? If you look at your drawings later, can you remember details about the lesson?" This might also take the form of a think aloud on the teacher's part. "I use metaphors and analogies to help me think through concepts. One example is to compare the writing of a paper to building a house. First, the structure (floors, walls, roof) needs to be built. Then, the details (light fixtures, appliances, furniture) are added." Self-reflection is difficult and needs to be modeled and scaffolded just like any new skill.

## CONSIDERATIONS

There are many considerations to keep in mind when thinking about ways to represent new information to students.

## Maintaining High Expectations

When student teachers are creating lesson plans and learning to differentiate for students' needs, one mistake they often make is to lower or "water down" the expectations for some students. For example, one student teacher was writing a lesson for which the objective was to learn multiplication of two-digit numerals. When asked how she would differentiate for students who struggled, she responded by creating a modified objective of multiplying one-digit numerals or very simple two-digit numerals (e.g., $10 \times 10$). What happens in a case such as this is that all students are able to complete the task set in front of them, so it seems that all students are successful in reaching the objective of the lesson. However, they are not. Some students are deprived of the opportunity to reach the same objective as their classmates. So what should be done instead? Rather than sticking to the same instruction and changing the objective, stick to the same objective and change the instruction. Provide various materials, such as manipulatives, graphic organizers, or a checklist of steps, while breaking down the process into several smaller chunks. Some students will be able to complete a few chunks together, and others may need to work through each small step to arrive at the answer. This provides supports without creating a glass ceiling. This is an example of UDL if every student has the opportunity to use and choose from all of the materials and supports provided. The idea of universal representations is that every way is for everyone.

## Learning Styles

One of the educational theories naturally linked to the input of information is learning style theory. There is currently a strong debate in the field about the existence and research base of learning styles. Proponents of learning style theory assert that all students have different styles for perceiving and processing new information. Translated into classroom practice, this means that teachers would determine each student's learning style and present information in each one's preferred modality. Various theorists have proposed models and assessments of learning styles (e.g., Dunn, Dunn, & Price, 1984; Honey & Mumford, 2006; Kolb, 1984).

Opponents of learning style theory assert that there is no evidence that learning styles exist (Riener & Willingham, 2010). Rather than teaching students in their best modalities, teachers should teach in the content's best modality; meaning, certain types of information are best presented in certain modalities—visual, auditory, or kinesthetic (Willingham, 2005).

Acknowledging this debate is useful, but not as useful as focusing on what will support the greatest number of students toward obtaining access to, perceiving, processing, and comprehending the greatest amount of content. There are ideas that both sides agree on: Students are different, and those differences should be taken into account; students have different interests; and students have different background knowledge and experience (Riener & Willingham, 2010).

If we focus too intently on determining a student's learning style, it can become another way of labeling and categorizing students. Input is about access, not labeling or categorizing. It is about bringing meaning to a concept and strengthening the connections. Teachers are meaning-makers. Good teaching—inclusive, universally designed teaching— is not offering visual input for visual learners, auditory input for auditory learners, and kinesthetic input for kinesthetic learners. Good teaching is offering multiple input for every learner. The teacher's role is to discover how to effectively represent content in different ways and formats. The strategies in this section are a start to the possibilities.

## How It All Comes Together

One of the foundational axioms of integrating UbD and DI is that teachers provide multiple opportunities for students to explore, interpret, apply, shift perspectives, empathize, and self-assess. This includes the ideas that students should be supported in thinking in complex ways, students differ in their levels of sophistication with any concept, understanding results from meaningful interaction with ideas, and teachers who use more modes of presentation reach more students. Teachers who teach all students use a variety of strategies to actively engage students in learning and allow them to address readiness levels, interests, and learning needs, while helping students understand which strategies work best for them (Tomlinson & McTighe, 2006).

Gay (2010) asserted that matching teaching styles with learning styles is a way to build bridges among cultures and build inclusive communities of learning. As well, varied formats of instruction reach more learners. Teachers who provide multiple opportunities for learning maintain high expectations, have knowledge of cultural differences, and use that knowledge to create effective teaching and learning opportunities. In other words, teaching in one way is not responsive.

In terms of input, brain-based research has a lot to tell us. Essentially, multiple representations mean better memory and learning (Willis, 2006). If the brain is introduced to a concept in multiple ways, it will store the experience in multiple places. The more places in the brain that store the information, the more interconnectedness and cross-referencing there is, so the data is learned, not just memorized. "That is the reason for teaching important material through multiple learning pathways such as several senses (hearing, seeing, touching) as well as through several subjects (cross-curricular topics)" (Willis, 2006, p. 5).

Kliewer (1998) has agreed on the importance of multiple representations of information in any child's environment. The ways that children view the world are by no means objective or the same for every child. Each child's mind is dynamic, changing, and evolving as he or she interacts with the surrounding environment. They reform knowledge and skills with each interaction. When this is recognized, all children in their uniqueness can be valued as full citizens.

# Food, Drinks, and Gum

**Allow drinks, snacks, and gum chewing any time.** In class?! Yes, in class—whenever the students need it. The hardest part about this strategy is getting over the idea that snacking and gum chewing are not allowed in class. Why can't they be? Many elementary classrooms have a designated snack time, but not all students need a snack at the same time. Children and teens vary greatly in their size, activity level, and metabolism. It is difficult for a student to concentrate and learn if he or she is thinking more about satisfying the basic need of hunger. A middle or high schooler may be able to grab a granola bar (if available) between classes, but in elementary school, students are at the mercy of the lunch or snack schedule. Gum chewing should also be allowed and encouraged, especially for students who would otherwise chew their nails or pencils. Gum chewing does not distract from learning; it actually enhances it! Smith (2010) found that gum chewing is associated with greater alertness, more positive mood, and improved selective and sustained attention.

**Try This**

Food, drinks, and gum

Beth Jackelen, a fourth-grade teacher, has responded to her students' diverse needs in terms of snacks by allowing them to nibble whenever needed. She also keeps a coffee pot of hot water available at the sink so that students can make a cup of cocoa or instant soup. Because cocoa and soup packets are nonperishable, she stores up contributions and keeps them handy in case students find themselves without a snack.

## Why This Works

- **Research base.** Maslow's hierarchy of needs tells us that basic physiological needs must be fulfilled before higher needs (Maslow, Frager, & Fadiman, 1987).

- **Student involvement.** Likely the biggest argument against drinks, snacks, and gum in class is the potential for mess. Rather than remove the opportunity to protect the classroom's cleanliness, teach the students and involve them in mess prevention and cleaning.

- **Reasonable use.** Stockpiling nonperishable snacks and gum is important so that no one goes without. Keeping a hot pot of water ready is simple. It takes little time each morning to set up and can also be part of students' jobs.

- **Expectations maintained.** Another common argument against this practice is that the students will abuse the privilege. Students should be expected to use only as needed and to get their work done at the same time. If a student is not getting work done because he or she is always in the sink or snack area, the problem is not the sink or snack area. The problem is that the student is looking for something more engaging.

- **Equity and universality.** Some families can and will contribute more than others toward the class store, but anything contributed by anyone strengthens the whole. As long as specialty snacks are kept for students with particular dietary needs, everyone is supported.

→ **IF . . . THEN** ←

If gum chewing is used to improve response time and performance in testing situations, then this can also be a strategy for **Assessment.**

ASSESSMENT

# Nooks

**Create nooks.** A nook is any individual space that affords a private and quiet area for studying, reading, assessment, or taking a break. Nooks can be created by purchasing or creating desktop study carrels or by rearranging furniture to zone off a certain area of the room. Not every student will need to use a nook, but having nooks to choose when needed is important for any inclusive classroom. Stocking these areas with materials needed for the purpose—books, paper, and writing tools or pillows and fidget toys—will create an inviting space where students can learn and/or rejuvenate, rather than feel excluded.

**Try This**

Reading nook

## Why This Works

- **Research base.** Golden (2012) and Kluth and Danaher (2010) spoke about the benefits of zoned areas for individual space.

- **Student involvement.** Students can help design and create nooks and zones. If students have the opportunity to reflect on what they need in the space and when and how the space should be used appropriately, then they will see the space as a learning strategy.

- **Reasonable use.** Commercial study carrels are sturdy but can be expensive. Simply moving furniture or creating a divider out of cardboard is inexpensive (or free!) and offers the same benefits.

- **Expectations maintained.** Students who use the individual spaces are not excused from work; they are offered a supportive place to complete the work or to refresh so that they can return to work.

- **Equity and universality.** Everyone should have the choice to use a study carrel or move to a nook. The choice should always be the student's. The teacher should never insist that a student use the area as a punishment or time-out. Then, it becomes exclusionary.

> ▶ IF . . . THEN ◀
>
> If nooks and calming spaces that reduce visual distractions or sensory input are used to help a student better focus and engage in the lesson, then this can also be a strategy for **Engagement.**
>
> ENGAGEMENT
>
>

#  Visually Accessible Text

**Provide visually accessible reading materials.** For students with vision loss, sans serif fonts (i.e., without small lines tailing from the edges of the letters) and fonts that are proportionally spaced are often recommended. However, other research has indicated that for some types of vision loss, particularly macular degeneration, Courier font may be best because of the wider spacing, even though it is a serif font (i.e., has small lines tailing from the edges of the letters). Which ones should be used? Simple—the one(s) that the student decides is best. Experiment with various fonts in various sizes. Then, have the preferred ones available at all times for all materials.

 **Try This**

Visually accessible text

## Why This Works

- **Research base.** Tarita-Nistor, Lam, Brent, Steinbach, and Gonzalez (2013) reported a study of the effectiveness of various fonts, determining Courier to be the best for age-related macular degeneration. A small-scale version of this study can be done in the classroom, in collaboration with vision specialists, checking acuity and strain.

- **Student involvement.** Students should be involved in assessing which materials are best. Then, they can self-manage their reading materials in terms of advocating for their availability in all classes or creating them on the computer.

- **Reasonable use.** Any written material can be printed in a different font and size. Hardcopy materials can be scanned or photocopied and enlarged.

- **Expectations maintained.** Changing the appearance of the material does not change the student's independence in decoding, comprehending, and applying the reading—in fact, it enhances it!

- **Equity and universality.** Think about material preparation in a different way—instead of small font for most of the class and specialized for one or two students, create all worksheets in the larger, clearer font size needed for the student(s) with visual impairments. Then, everyone can use any of the papers in the stack.

> → IF . . . THEN ←
>
> If visually accessible text is used so that the teacher can more accurately evaluate a student's independent reading level, then this can also be a strategy for **Assessment.**
>
> ASSESSMENT
>
>

# Auditory Books

**Provide accessible reading materials such as auditory books.** Auditory books, whether they are books that have been recorded on tape or talking books such as those created by Leapfrog, are beneficial for students with vision loss but also for students whose stronger modality for processing information is auditory. Auditory books can be used with just the sound or used with the pictures or words accompanied by sound to reinforce more than one mean of input.

Audio books

## Why This Works

- **Research base.** Hobbs (2007) discussed the benefits of audio books, including ability to comprehend, make inferences, and engage in critical thinking.

- **Student involvement.** With access to a listening center, e-reader, or computer station during reading times, students can choose to use audio books or written books.

- **Reasonable use.** Teachers can make tapes or CDs to go along with any book or material in the classroom simply by making their own voice recording. Audio books are available online.

- **Expectations maintained.** There are common myths that audio books encourage students to be lazy and fall behind in skills by not reading on their own. Actually, audio books increase listening skills, improve correct use of punctuation, and engage students in the reading process. Accountability for comprehending and applying the content is the same.

- **Equity and universality.** With the choice available to all students and use of headphones encouraged, everyone can have access to materials in ways that increase comprehension.

> ▶ IF . . . THEN ◀
>
> If audio books are used to motivate students to interact with text in a different way, then this can also be a strategy for **Engagement.**
>
> ENGAGEMENT
>
>

# Tactile Books

**Provide accessible reading materials such as tactile and multisensory books.** In addition to seeing and hearing a story, an important means for input is to use the tactile sense as well. Braille is one way, but other types of texture can be added to any book. Cut the pages apart, add anything—pipe cleaners, wiki sticks, cotton balls, textured felt, beads, rice, puff paint—to focus on certain words, pictures, or concepts. Add paper clips to the edges of the paper for easier turning for fingers with limited dexterity. If you also record the book on tape or CD, you have a multisensory book!

**Try This**

Tactile books

**Bag Books** (http://www.bagbooks.org) are brilliant kits that offer accessible stories for students in need to interact through actions and emotions rather than words and pictures. Each kit includes a large storyboard with 6–12 lines of text and specially selected objects that can be accessed hand-over-hand or engaged through sight, sound, touch, smell, and motion (e.g., a pom-pom to simulate shaking tree branches, a handheld pump to create wind). There are also guides to a multisensory approach to novels.

## Why This Works

- **Research base.** Stockall, Dennis, and Miller (2012) emphasized the need for teachers to provide visual, auditory, and tactile input to provide greater opportunity to interact with materials.

- **Student involvement.** Using a multisensory book can be as independent as reading text. Students should have the opportunity to reflect on the difference when reading or listening to a story while touching it!

- **Reasonable use.** Adding texture to books is simple, but creating more than a handful is time-consuming and may get expensive.

- **Expectations maintained.** Comprehension and application of the materials is not changed. The various means of input support learning.

- **Equity and universality.** Universality here is shifting the way we think about reading and learning from texts and other materials. It does not always mean seeing the written word.

→ IF . . . THEN ←

If tactile books are used to help a student make a connection to the book and sustain his or her interaction with the book over time, then this can also be a strategy for **Engagement.**

ENGAGEMENT

# Self-Amplifiers

**Provide self-amplifiers.** Some students need to hear information out loud to better process it. Self-talk has many advantages in literacy development and effective processing of input; however, it can be distracting when others in the classroom are working quietly. Self-amplifiers or listening tubes (some brands include WhisperPhone, Speak'N Hear, and Toobaloo) allow speakers to hear themselves loud and clear even when they are whispering softly.

Toobaloo

## Why This Works

- **Research base.** Self-amplifiers improve signal-to-noise ratio to enhance the auditory feedback loop for self-monitoring and self-correcting or reading, spelling, and articulation (Rasinski, Flexer, & Szypulski, 2006).

- **Student involvement.** Students should try activities with and without self-amplifiers to decide if they are helpful.

- **Reasonable use.** Self-amplifiers can be electronic or acoustic. Acoustic ones, such as those listed previously, do not need circuitry, so they are much less expensive and easier to use and manage. They can also be homemade out of PVC tubing from any plumbing supply store, by connecting two small elbow-shaped pieces together.

- **Expectations maintained.** Students are learning the same information aurally. They are also learning another way in which they can create a classroom environment where everyone's needs are met—those who need to self-talk can do so without disturbing those who need quiet.

- **Equity and universality.** Everyone gets to use them. Each student should have his or her own tube, with extras available in an accessible spot.

> ➤ IF . . . THEN ◄
>
> If listening tubes are used so that students can self-assess their reading and speaking skills, then this can also be a strategy for **Assessment.**
>
> ASSESSMENT

# Schedules

**Create classroom schedule variations.** An agenda helps frame the day for everyone. There are many different ways to display the daily schedule or agenda so that everyone can use and apply it. Golden (2012) shared a fantastic example that incorporates needed information in several ways. A vertical chart with four columns displays the time in two ways (analog and digital) and the event in two ways (text and picture). Once each event is past, a "finished" sign is placed over the event. In addition to an enlarged schedule such as this posted in the classroom, individual students could have customized schedules taped to their desks with text, icons, pictures, and braille that depict events unique to that student.

**Try This**

Class schedule

## Why This Works

- **Research base.** A clear, predictable schedule of the school day cultivates student productivity and greater opportunity for learning (Kamps, 2002).

- **Student involvement.** The schedules should be interactive. Students should be able to assemble the daily schedule themselves and check off events, remove events, and post the "finished" signs as the day progresses.

- **Reasonable use.** The only costs associated with the handmade schedules are for materials (e.g., poster board, Velcro) and laminating. They require time ahead to make the event units and times.

- **Expectations maintained.** Expectations of students can be increased. They now have a way to manage their own time.

- **Equity and universality.** The schedule variation described by Golden (2012) can be accessed by readers and nonreaders, novice and advanced time-tellers. It meets the needs of students who need the predictability of what is coming next and how long it will last.

→ IF . . . THEN ←

If schedules are used to relieve students' stress about what to expect in the daily schedule so that they can be more productive, then this can also be a strategy for **Output.**

OUTPUT

# Syn-naps

**Take Syn-naps.** Whew! We have been busy. The neurons in our brains have been releasing neurotransmitters to carry information to the next neuron in order to create a pathway of new knowledge. It is time for a brain rest. Brains need naps like bodies need naps. Willis (2006) used the term *syn-naps* to describe the periodic rests needed to replenish neurotransmitters and allow executive functions to process information. One- to two-minute breaks should be worked into lessons about every 15 minutes. Simply have students move, stretch, sing, dance, or use the bathroom, then sit back down. Once the break is over, be sure to help the students make a meaningful connection to the material just learned so that they can move it from their working memory to their long-term memory. For example, "How are input strategies like vitamins?"

## Try This

When Jamie Nells, a fifth-grade teacher, notices his students losing focus, he has them "touch the tree." The tree is across the schoolyard. He is lucky enough to have an exit near his classroom from which he can see the tree and students at all times. It takes the whole class less than 3 minutes to touch the tree and return to the lesson, rejuvenated.

## Why This Works

- **Research base.** When neurotransmitters are depleted, students become restless and distracted. If a break is not given, stress can build up in the amygdala and block processing of new information and storage of new information (Willis, 2006).

- **Student involvement.** Students can be in charge of when they need a break. One of the class jobs assigned can be Amygdala Regulator, a student who signals for a break every 15 minutes or when he or she notices fidgety behavior.

- **Reasonable use.** Breaks are free and do not require special training, but the solidifying activity does require knowledge of lesson closure techniques and must be planned and ready when the break ends.

- **Expectations maintained.** Some teachers may feel like frequent breaks take away from time on task, but really they increase the quality of time on task a great deal. Mr. Nells attests to this.

- **Equity and universality.** Everyone needs a break and should be given one even if his or her work is not done. Denying a break should *never* be used as a consequence in the classroom. That would be the same as withholding teaching or learning opportunities. Also, make sure everyone has the support he or she needs to participate in the break if you choose to do a physical activity (e.g., stretching, yoga, touching the tree).

**IF . . . THEN**

If syn-naps are used to help maintain positive emotional states, then this can also be a strategy for **Engagement.**

ENGAGEMENT

# 10:2 Theory

**Employ the 10:2 theory to increase new learning.** Similar to syn-naps, the 10:2 theory (Rutherford, 2002) is based on the idea that a break or pause should be introduced during instruction at regular intervals so that new information can be processed before it is lost. When planning your lesson and pacing, make sure that for every 10 minutes of instruction, you allow 2 minutes of processing time. You can prompt the processing time by having students share one new idea with a classmate, write one sentence or question about the new information, draw an illustration, find a pattern, and so forth. Lesson plans and note sheets can be structured to scaffold this.

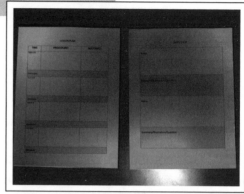

10:2 theory (shaded rows show processing time)

## Why This Works

- **Research base.** Two minutes of processing time every 10 minutes can counteract the mental lapses that occur when short-term memory overloads, an idea is not grasped right away, information in the lesson is incongruent with prior experience, or students are distracted (Rutherford, 2002).

- **Student involvement.** Students can remind the teacher that they need processing time or suggest ideas for thinking about the information that was just covered.

- **Reasonable use.** This strategy entails very little planning time. Once you have created a list of 2-minute review ideas, you just need to plan to use one at each 10-minute interval of your lesson plan.

- **Expectations maintained.** Students should be expected to use the processing time to stay on task.

- **Equity and universality.** Providing choice in the way that the processing time is used responds to each student's needs.

**IF . . . THEN**

If the structured note sheets and time provided are used to allow students to express their current understanding, then this can also be a strategy for **Output.**

OUTPUT

# FM-Adapted Computer Stations

**Provide hearing aid adapter cords at every computer and listening station in the classroom.** Students who wear hearing aids and use FM amplification systems in the classroom are not able to wear traditional headsets when working on computers or listening stations. Rather, the student typically uses an adapter cord that plugs into the computer and into the amplifier. Thus, everything that is audible on the computer or listening station is amplified and directed right to the hearing aids. If you have an adapter cord at every computer and every listening station, then every station is universal.

**Try This**

Adapter cords

## Why This Works

- **Research base.** An adapter cord is an effective assistive technology specifically designed to make use of the computer or listening station universal. It is an example of UDL because it reduces barriers to learning and facilitates perception of the information by all learners (CAST, 2011).

- **Student involvement.** Students can evaluate the effectiveness of using the adapter cords for their hearing aids at each station and the benefits of working with different students regardless of which computer is used.

- **Reasonable use.** The teacher and/or students can make sure each station is equipped for all. Once this is done, the teacher does not have to think about which student must be assigned to which station.

- **Expectations maintained.** No work is done for any student. It provides access for all students to input the same information and apply it to the same standard of mastery.

- **Equity and universality.** If only one station in the classroom has an adapter cord, then the student with hearing aids does not have a choice of which station to use, whereas all of the other students do have that choice. If all stations can be used universally, then all students have equitable choice and opportunity.

**→ IF . . . THEN ←**

If adapter cords are used so that students can use the computer or listening station to express learning or create a product of their learning, then this can also be a strategy for **Output.**

OUTPUT

# Digital Text or E-books

**Have a library of digital texts or e-books.** There are many software programs and web sites that offer digital texts or e-books. E-books can be adapted to meet the various needs of students in ways that printed text cannot. Text can be enlarged, read aloud, highlighted, or bolded. Words can be hyperlinked to a dictionary to provide immediate definitions. Students can add notes or drawings, save or print them, and then clean the page for the next reader. Some great resources include

E-books

- Boardmaker: http://www.mayer-johnson.com/boardmaker-software (Users can create print materials using Picture Exchange Communication Symbols [PECS] or other symbols and graphics on this site.)

- Bookshare: https://www.bookshare.org (This site includes accessible books and materials adapted for print disabilities.)

- BrainPOP: http://www.brainpop.com (This site provides animated videos about curricular content concepts.)

- CAST UDL Book Builder: http://bookbuilder.cast.org (Users can read, create, and share digital books on this site.)

- NaturalReader: http://www.naturalreaders.com (The software provided on this site reads any text aloud.)

- Signed Stories: http://www.signedstories.com (Books on this site can be viewed in sign language with subtitles.)

- Tumble Book Cloud: http://www.tumblebookcloud.com (This site has an extensive library of e-books.)

- Word Talk: http://www.wordtalk.org.uk/Home (This site provides a text-to-speech plug-in.)

Maggie Driscoll, an elementary school teacher, has created her own e-books. She creates or collects pictures, adds text, then places each page on a PowerPoint slide so it can be viewed from any device (e.g., iPad, computer, interactive whiteboard). She can customize the text or use Boardmaker to insert picture symbols to meet various needs. Adaptive switches ensure that all students are able to turn the "pages" on the computer.

*(continued)*

# Why This Works

- **Research base.** Multimedia technologies such as e-books provide a myriad of tools that enable teachers to meet individualized needs, unlike text on paper. These new options, when planned carefully, facilitate learning, reduce frustration, and increase engagement (Pisha & Coyne, 2001).

- **Student involvement.** Computers allow students to adapt the materials themselves, without having to rely on teachers to complete the time-consuming task of modifying printed materials.

- **Reasonable use.** The technology needed, both hardware and software, may be expensive. Most classrooms have at least one computer, but more may be needed to be sure each student has access. Once purchased, most programs have tutorials and are easily learned by the teacher and students with reasonable time commitment. The best programs are universally designed to be intuitive in their use.

- **Expectations maintained.** Through e-books, students gain literacy skills and content knowledge, as well as technological ability.

- **Equity and universality.** Computer hardware adaptations and software responsiveness to user needs, ability levels, and learning rates make digital text and e-books much more accessible and equitable than traditional print materials. Remember, all of these are for all students—even Signed Stories are beneficial for hearing students because learning ASL is a skill for everyone!

If e-books are used so that teachers can evaluate literacy skills outside the confines of static text on paper, which does not accommodate learning difficulties (Pisha & Coyne, 2001), then this can also be a strategy for **Assessment.**

ASSESSMENT

# ·◻· Note-Taking Hardware and Software

**Provide a note-taking pen and Notability.** There are two technological strategies to support notetaking. The first is assistive technology hardware—a note-taking pen, such as the wireless Smart Pen by Livescribe (http://www.livescribe.com/en-us), records everything the student writes and hears during a lesson. Later, the student can tap anywhere in the notes and replay the audio from that portion of the lesson. All notes and recording are automatically stored wirelessly for future use. They can be accessed anywhere and anytime you can access the Internet.

A software support is a note-taking app, such as Notability (available through iTunes). Notability allows the user to take notes by using handwriting, PDF annotation, typing, recording, graphics, drawing, and/ or highlighting, so notes are most meaningful to the person taking them. Also, like the note-taking pen, the device used (e.g., iPad or iPhone) can record the lesson, so tapping on the section of notes plays back the audio too.

**Try This**

Notability on iPad

## Why This Works

- **Research base.** In one study, Higgins and Raskind (2005) found that a note-taking pen increased reading comprehension and accuracy in students with learning disabilities.

- **Student involvement.** Students can customize notes and reflect on what best helps them review the content of the lesson (e.g., the audio recording, the written notes, drawings).

- **Reasonable use.** Note-taking pens can be expensive. The top-rated pens range from about $30 to $300. The Notabality app is about $3, but the devices needed for the app are expensive, ranging from $300 to $800.

- **Expectations maintained.** The note-taking support should enhance the lesson, not distract from it. The student is still required to review the notes and learn the material.

*(continued)*

Input Through Technology: Note-Taking Hardware and Software 79

- **Equity and universality.** This technology supports students who have difficulty taking thorough written notes while listening to a lesson or studying from written notes. It provides the content to be reviewed in auditory or picture form in one step.

**→ IF . . . THEN ←**

If note-taking software and hardware is used so that a student can sustain attention on a lesson if precious energy is not focused on difficult notetaking, then this can also be a strategy for **Engagement.**

ENGAGEMENT

# Access to Auditory Input

**Offer multiple supports when using any auditory input.** Students with hearing loss should have access to all of the auditory information in the classroom. There are several ways to accomplish this through assistive technology:

- *Personal amplifiers:* These are handheld amplifiers that can be used by anyone with hearing aids or even just with ear buds.

- *FM amplification systems:* The system consists of an amplifier (about the size of a cell phone) that the teacher wears on a belt clip or lanyard and receivers (about 1 cm cube) that clip to the base of the student's hearing aids. These are customized for individual students and programmed to their specific hearing loss. Some amplifiers can be connected to multiple students.

Access to auditory input

- *Whole-school loop systems:* These systems consist of a microphone, an amplifier, and a loop wire. Once wire is looped around an area (e.g., the perimeter of the classroom), any sounds from the area are picked up, amplified, and sent to hearing aids. Unlike FM systems, they are great for group settings because they do not just amplify the voice of the teacher wearing the device.

- *Closed-captioning or subtitling:* On any visual media display, this translates the auditory information into text. It might be a direct translation or a summary of information, and/or include a description of nonspeech sounds (e.g., "door slams").

- *Instant translation devices:* These instant messaging devices, such as Interpretype, help facilitate face-to-face communication with individuals who are deaf, deafblind, or hard of hearing when one or more participants do not use sign language.

- *Voice recognition software:* These software packages are used to immediately translate speech to written text. If the screen is displayed to the whole classroom, whatever speech the computer picks up can be translated to text and displayed to everyone.

## Why This Works

- **Research base.** This is an issue of equal access as much as it is an issue of learning. The Individuals with Disabilities Education Improvement Act (IDEA) of 2004 (PL 108-446) ensures that students who are deaf or hard of hearing have supports needed to learn. Section 504 of the Rehabilitation Act of 1973 (PL 93-112) ensures supports for any student with an

*(continued)*

impairment that limits a major life activity (e.g., hearing auditory stimuli in the classroom). All students ideologically have the right to have access to all input in the classroom that anyone else can, including lessons, the school loudspeaker, assemblies, side conversations, student responses in discussion, everything.

- **Student involvement.** Over time, students should become increasingly aware of the input that is in the classroom and whether or not it can be accessed by everyone. If not, each student as a member of an inclusive classroom has a responsibility to make sure it is accessible by creating visuals or always using the ones available. It is not just the teacher's job. It is everyone's job to include everyone.

- **Reasonable use.** Technology is expensive, plain and simple. Computer hardware and software, hearing aids, amplification and looping systems are all costly, and training for maintenance and effective use is necessary. The most cost-effective systems would be those that provide access to the most people.

- **Expectations maintained.** Students who have access to all input can be held accountable for all input. If they do not have access, they have less opportunity to learn what their peers are learning.

- **Equity and universality.** The idea is to strive to go beyond individual supports and make all aspects of the classroom accessible to everyone. With whole-school looping systems, students have greater access than with FM amplification systems. Though not technology, it is the same with ASL—a one-to-one interpreter differentiates for one individual, but ASL instruction for all students and staff creates a universally designed environment.

→ IF . . . THEN ←

If these strategies for access to auditory input are used so that students can have access to all testing information, then this can also be a strategy for **Assessment.**

ASSESSMENT

# Access to Visual Input

**Offer multiple supports when using any visual input.** For students with vision loss, there are many assistive technology supports to provide equitable access to visuals:

- *Talking resources and equipment:* Examples include calculators, whiteboards, and photo albums.

- *Audio description on movies:* Along the lines of closed-captioning, this describes all relevant visual information from the media source in detail.

- *Screen readers:* These software programs are designed to read and describe web pages to computer users.

  Here are a few helpful web sites:

- The Audio Description Project: http://www.acb.org/adp/accessibility.html

- LS&S (Learning, Sight, and Sound): http://www.lssproducts.com

- School Specialty: https://store.schoolspecialty.com

Access to visual input

 ## Why This Works

- **Research base.** This is an issue of equal access as much as it is an issue of learning. IDEA 2004 ensures that students who are blind or have vision loss have supports needed to learn. Section 504 of the Rehabilitation Act of 1973 ensures supports for any student with an impairment that limits a major life activity (e.g., seeing visual stimuli in the classroom). All students ideologically have the right to have access to all input in the classroom that anyone else can, including lessons, the school loudspeaker, assemblies, side conversations, and student responses in discussion—everything.

- **Student involvement.** Over time, students should become increasingly aware of the input that is in the classroom and whether or not it can be accessed by everyone. If not, each student as a member of an inclusive classroom has a responsibility to make sure it is accessible. It is not just the teacher's job. It is everyone's job to include everyone.

- **Reasonable use.** These items of assistive technology vary in price.

  *Audio description on movies:* Free when available

  *Screen reader software:* $92.80–$895.00

*(continued)*

*Talk Boards from School Specialty:* $94.99 for a set of 12

*Talking calculator from LS&S:* $11.95–$249.95

*Talking Photo Album from School Specialty:* $35.99

- **Expectations maintained.** Students who have access to all input can be held accountable for all input. If they do not have access, they have less opportunity to learn what their peers are learning.

- **Equity and universality.** The idea is to strive to go beyond individual supports and make all aspects of the classroom accessible to everyone.

→ IF ... THEN ←

If these strategies for access to visual input are used so that students can have access to all testing information, then this can also be a strategy for **Assessment.**

ASSESSMENT

INPUT

# ·⌐∩· Peer-Mediated Instruction

**Use peer-mediated instruction.** Students who have difficulty reading texts independently will have more difficulty forming new concepts. Peer-mediated instruction (also called reciprocal teaching, classwide peer tutoring, or peer-assisted strategies) is based on students coaching one another through the decoding of reading materials, questioning one another on the content to clarify and make sense of the new information, helping one another summarize the ideas, and cocreating reading notes.

Here are two helpful web sites:

- Kagan Catalog, Cooperative Learning: http://www .kaganonline.com/catalog/cooperative_learning.php

- National Center on Accessible Instructional Materials: http://aim.cast.org/learn/historyarchive/ backgroundpapers/peer-mediated_instruction

**Try This**

Peer-mediated instruction

## Why This Works

- **Research base.** Peer-mediated instruction is structured to provide scaffolds for students to construct new meaning and integrate new concepts (Kroeger, Burton, & Preston, 2009).

- **Student involvement.** When used effectively, cooperative learning and peer-mediated instruction allows students to monitor their own thinking and progress when teachers are not available because the framework supports independent interaction.

- **Reasonable use.** There is no cost involved, but preparation time is needed. Teachers should research the process of establishing well-structured peer-mediation. It will take time to teach and scaffold the skills with students. Students will not just begin to teach each other.

- **Expectations maintained.** Once groups are established, students are expected to support each other without giving each other the answers or doing the work for one another. Students learn content, learning strategies, and collaboration skills.

- **Equity and universality.** Content-area textbooks that are geared to a particular grade level often present difficulties because students vary a great deal in their reading levels. In peer-mediated instruction, all students work together through material toward new learning.

→ IF . . . THEN ◄

If peer-mediated instruction is used so that students are motivated by working with each other, independently from the teacher, then this can also be a strategy for **Engagement.**

ENGAGEMENT

# Study Snippets

**Use brief study snippet videos to reinforce learning.** Study Snippets are simply short (this is the key!), teacher-made videos that summarize a lesson by reviewing the main concept in a fun and catchy way—by singing or rapping a song, reciting a poem, selling a strategy, or showing a visual. For students who need repetition, repetition, repetition, this allows them to review as many times as needed.

**Must-read**

Kluth, P., & Danaher, S. (2010). *From tutor scripts to talking sticks: 100 ways to differentiate instruction in K–12 inclusive classrooms.* Baltimore, MD: Paul H. Brookes Publishing Co.

Study snippets

 ## Why This Works

- **Research base.** Kluth and Danaher (2010) expounded on effective ways to use what they call "curriculum commercials" to teach reading skills and academic content.

- **Student involvement.** Once the videos are created, students can play the videos on their own—in classroom centers, on their home computers, or on televisions with DVD players. Then, they can make their own!

- **Reasonable use.** You need a video camera and a computer with a DVD burner and/or media software. You may already have a phone that records good-quality videos. If not, video cameras range in price from $5.95 for single-use to $399 for a high-quality zoom or flip camera.

- **Expectations maintained.** This does not change any content taught. It simply provides another way to reinforce it.

- **Equity and universality.** All auditory and visual supports used in the classroom should apply to these videos as well!

➤ **IF . . . THEN** ◄

If Study Snippets are used as a unique, media-based strategy so that students have a fun, memorable way to study, then this can also be a strategy for **Engagement.**

ENGAGEMENT

**86**                                    Input Through Content Instruction: Study Snippets

# Responsive Resource Posters

**Create and display culturally responsive resource posters.** Classrooms often sport many posters on the walls to be used as resources for students—mnemonics, checklists, alphabet charts, word walls. Instead of using commercial posters that are not tailored to your own students, create ones that are meaningful to them. For example, alphabet charts should have photos of what the students know. Instead of a cartoon picture of a xylophone, for example, students would relate much better to a photo of their classmate, Xander!

### Try This

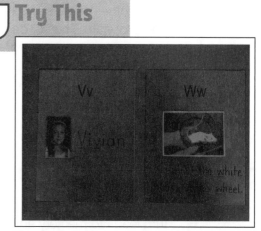

Resource posters

## Why This Works

- **Research base.** Gay (2002) identified three types of curricula: formal curricula (textbooks and district-approved materials), symbolic curricula (posters, bulletin boards, awards, school displays), and societal curricula (media portrayal). It is important for all three to be culturally responsive.

- **Student involvement.** Students should be fully involved in the creation of posters and other wall hangings in the classroom. Photos of themselves and their families should be included; their words and voices should be reflected.

- **Reasonable use.** At most, you need poster board and laminating material for long-term wear and tear. Most often, teachers simply use chart paper and markers.

- **Expectations maintained.** Resource posters in the classroom are innately scaffolding. They are available for those who need it and nonintrusive for those who do not. They are an additional reinforcement of content learned by all.

- **Equity and universality.** Make sure the resource posters are accessible to all, just like any other printed material in the classroom. Miniature versions can be affixed to students' desks for easier reference.

> **→ IF . . . THEN ←**
>
> If responsive resource posters are used so that students can make meaningful connections with the content when they see themselves and their culture in the materials, then this can also be a strategy for **Engagement.**
>
> ENGAGEMENT
>
>

# Humor

**Use humor to anchor new content.** Humor can be the comprehension connection that some students need to make sense of and store new information. Added to other visual, auditory, and tactile content and used appropriately, humor can be a powerful learning tool. Some ideas to use are games, parodies, comical voices, wigs and hats, puns, oxymorons, alliteration, and acronyms.

## Try This

Humor

## Why This Works

- **Research base.** Humor is arousing, which leads to student interest and focus, which in turn leads to memory and increased learning. When teachers use humor, students learn more (Wanzer, 2002).

- **Student involvement.** Students can reflect on what they learned about the content connected to humor and whether it is an effective strategy for them. Students should also be encouraged to create their own jokes about a topic.

- **Reasonable use.** Humor can be used at any time with any subject, but time should be taken to plan the humor used so that it is most appropriate and not distracting from the content.

- **Expectations maintained.** Students not only learn the content but also appropriate use of humor. It is an important social skill and community-building exercise to recognize and apply humor that is fun for everyone.

- **Equity and universality.** Be respectful and politically correct at all times. Offensive humor may actually impede learning.

→ IF . . . THEN ←

If humor is used to motivate learning and build trust, then this can also be a strategy for **Engagement.**

ENGAGEMENT

#  Visualizing

**Build comprehension connections through visualizing techniques.** One way to help students understand new concepts is to help them visualize the ideas. Not the same as seeing the material, visualizing is creating images in the mind. This can be abstract, but McGregor (2007) shared many concrete ways to build this skill:

- Offer thinking stems, such as prompting students to think about what they see, hear, smell, taste, and feel about the topic.

- Play music to build mental images.

- Provide wordless books and ask students to describe the scenes.

- Prompt with mind-expanding questions such as, "What lies beyond the frame of the picture?"

 **Try This**

McGregor (2007) introduced the complex idea of visualizing by providing each student with a section of paper towel tube. After allowing them to explore the classroom through their new lens, she asked them to peer at an item of interest through the tube to trigger a memory or envision the item in a different context. The use of the tube scaffolds them toward visualizing when they read or write.

## Why This Works

- **Research base.** Visualization connects students personally with information because images are unique to each person, and engagement with information is deepened by creating images (McGregor, 2007).

- **Student involvement.** This is a great exercise in reflection. Students can create their own images and connect their own meanings.

- **Reasonable use.** This practice is free and simple.

- **Expectations maintained.** Expect more vivid descriptions and more questions about topics and readings!

- **Equity and universality.** Often students share what they visualize, but they should always have the choice not to share. Some of the most private memories make the most meaningful connections.

**→ IF . . . THEN ←**

If visualizing helps students write with greater and more descriptive detail, then this can also be a strategy for **Output.**

OUTPUT

---

# Continuum of Abstractness

**Scaffold communication with a continuum of abstractness.** Nonreaders or students with limited vocabulary can benefit from visuals of objects. This strategy offers a way to scaffold students from concrete to abstract representations, to support reading and communication skills. Golden (2012) described a five-part continuum:

**Try This**

1. The actual object is available to the student, paired with the spoken, signed, or written word.

2. A colored photo of the object is paired with the word.

3. A detailed, colored drawing is paired with the word.

Money continuum of abstractness

4. A simple black-and-white drawing or symbol is paired with the word.

5. Just the word is used.

## Why This Works

- **Research base.** This is supported by Piaget's (1952) theory of cognitive development from concrete to abstract thinking.

- **Student involvement.** Students should be involved in reflecting on parts of the continuum that is supportive. Scaffold them toward more abstract levels over time.

- **Reasonable use.** Creating this strategy entails finding actual objects and printing pictures, photos, and labels.

- **Expectations maintained.** This strategy illustrates the belief that students are always learning and advancing to the next step. This provides support for students in concrete thinking stages while challenging them gently toward the next level of abstractness.

- **Equity and universality.** The choice of all images and words can be displayed and available to everyone. This responds to all ability levels.

**IF . . . THEN**

If a continuum of abstractness is used to evaluate a student's application of the object separate from his or her written or spoken vocabulary, then this can also be a strategy for **Assessment.**

ASSESSMENT

# Accessible Presentation Software

**Make presentation software accessible to all ability levels.** Many teachers, particularly at the middle and high school levels, use presentation (slide show) software such as PowerPoint, Impress, or Key Note to deliver instruction. It is important to design slide shows so that all students can take part in the instructional setting. Doyle and Giangreco (2009) suggested the following:

- Make sure each slide is effective. Images should be of high quality. Always follow the 6 × 6 rule for text (6 lines maximum per slide, 6 words maximum per line). Include brief audio and video clips. Use contrasting colors that do not strain the eyes.

- Differentiate the slide shows for different users. Chunk information into shorter slide shows. Code certain slides as higher priority for individual students. Embed content-specific vocabulary and use any necessary visual or auditory supports.

- Allow choice in how the slides are printed (e.g., number of slides per page, color, design)

 **Try This**

**Powtoon free animated videos and presentations**
http://www.powtoon.com

**Prezi**
http://prezi.com

**Sliderocket**
http://www.sliderocket.com

**Visual Bee free presentation software**
http://www.visualbee.com/free/free-presentation-software.html

**YouTube video about making accessible PowerPoint presentations**
http://www.youtube.com/watch?v=-pb3vrEq-iU

 ## Why This Works

- **Research base.** Incorporating the ideas listed above when creating presentations facilitates the inclusion of students with intellectual disabilities in classroom instruction (Doyle & Giangreco, 2009).

- **Student involvement.** Students should be involved in deciding how the material should be coded (identifying which slides are high priority) and printed.

- **Reasonable use.** Software packages are available for both Mac and PC computers. Packages are available from $34.99 to $399.00. Free presentation software is available from Visual Bee, Powtoon, Google Docs, 280 Slides, Sliderocket, and Prezi.

- **Expectations maintained.** The objective for material to be learned is not modified; the curricular materials are adapted to be most accessible.

*(continued)*

- **Equity and universality.** Everyone in the classroom is receiving new information via instructional technology, which makes for an inclusive academic climate.

→ IF . . . THEN ←

If students can use presentation software to create slide shows that express their learning, then this can also be a strategy for **Output.**

OUTPUT

# Social Stories

**Use purchased or self-created Social Stories.**
In addition to academic content, sometimes students need support to learn about the complex social context of school. Many expectations for appropriate behaviors and reactions in certain situations are not directly taught. Social Stories can provide support needed. Social Stories are brief narratives that share accurate, meaningful information about a situation that helps students understand what is happening. They can be used for temporary events (e.g., substitute teacher, fire drills, change in daily schedule) or more complex long-term situations (e.g., divorce, moving, new sibling).

**Try This**

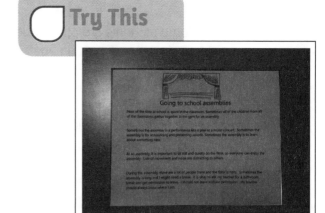

Social Stories

## Why This Works

- **Research base.** Gray (2010) described the benefits and purposes of Social Stories, addressed how to create your own Social Stories, and provided several prewritten stories.

- **Student involvement.** Students can be involved in deciding which Social Stories are needed.

- **Reasonable use.** Social Story resources are available from The Gray Center web site (http://www.thegraycenter.org), or you can create your own.

- **Expectations maintained.** Some students react in ways we do not expect given unpredictable or confusing situations. We need to support students in better understanding the situation, not try to train them to behave or react differently. We need to provide supports in the environment to meet their needs, not change the students. They are fine just the way they are.

- **Equity and universality.** All students should have access to Social Stories, particularly stories that have an impact on the whole class (e.g., fire drills). Everyone can benefit to some degree from better understanding unpredictable situations.

> **→ IF . . . THEN ←**
>
> If Social Stories are used to support more effective responses in certain situations as the students' comfort level increases, then this can also be a strategy for **Output.**
>
> OUTPUT
>
>

# Social Skill Autopsy

**Implement a social skill autopsy to teach new skills.** Some students are able to pick up on subtle social skills to determine appropriate behavior in a variety of settings. These students learn quickly and easily from mistakes so that they are not repeated. Other students have difficulty picking up on the many nuances of social expectations and may not be able to figure out what went wrong in a given situation in which they may have offended someone or otherwise acted inappropriately. The purpose of the social skill autopsy is to walk a student through this complex process by analyzing a specific social skill error and planning the behavioral options that could be implemented to improve interactions in the future. The steps to follow are to ask the student what happened, identify the mistakes made, assist in determining alternatives, share a similar scenario, and give social homework so that the student can practice in a real-life situation.

## Try This

Social skill autopsy

## Why This Works

- **Research base.** Lavoie (2005b) developed the social skill autopsy to be a structured, constructive, problem-solving strategy that provides an opportunity to learn in a realistic setting, as opposed to a punishment for unintentional errors. It is more effective than role playing, demonstrations, or theoretical discussions.

- **Student involvement.** Students are directly involved in all of the steps of this strategy. The student identifies the problem and the solutions.

- **Reasonable use.** This strategy does not involve formal training, but it does involve some preparation and familiarity with the method. Lavoie (2005b) is a great guide for implementation.

- **Expectations maintained.** All students should be expected to have appropriate social skills. If they have difficulty mastering them, the expectations should not be lowered; rather, the level of support should be raised.

- **Equity and universality.** Because this strategy is built around actual events, rather than theoretical scenarios, it is responsive to individual skill needs. It provides concrete, structured supports for any situation.

 IF . . . THEN

If social skill autopsies are used to provide students with several potential solutions for expressing themselves in social situations, then this can also be a strategy for **Output.**

OUTPUT

# Gaming Technology

**Use gaming technology as a therapeutic tool.** Students who have difficulty in complex social situations need opportunities to practice processing the situations and choosing their responses. An emerging way to provide this practice is through serious video game technology. One game that is currently under development, called *MindGamers in School,* allows players to develop avatars representing themselves, their strengths (Goal-Based Imp), and their problematic responses to school-related triggers (Problem-Based Imp). After populating the game world with player-selected triggers such as filth, social stressors, crowding, noise, and asymmetry, players navigate the virtual school using their stress level. This is accomplished by combining biofeedback training with player strengths and cognitive skills learned in therapy.

This is the innovative new therapeutic video game being developed at Rochester Institute of Technology (http://www.rit.edu/research/biox_story.php?id=105).

## Why This Works

- **Research base.** The game, although appealing to students' love of video games, incorporates many valuable therapeutic techniques: helping students better understand their behaviors and what sustains them, helping students develop a sense of hope and agency, and helping students develop coping strategies and skills (Jacobs, Rice, & Sugarman, 2012).

- **Student involvement.** Students were extensively involved in the development of this video game, so their needs are understood and met. In play, the students are in complete control, rehearsing strategies they have on hand and evaluating their own progress. All of the rewards and asset options in the game were determined based on student preferences.

- **Reasonable use.** Cost and availability of this particular game has not been determined.

- **Expectations maintained.** This video game builds on and integrates biofeedback, cognitive, and narrative approaches to working with restrictive and repetitive behaviors that can make it difficult for students to perform their best at school. The therapeutic goal is to help players develop and use their unique and innate coping strategies.

*(continued)*

- **Equity and universality.** Although plans to develop a home-based version of *MindGamers in School* are underway, access will initially be limited to those students who are working with a mental health professional. Those who would currently benefit most include teenagers who get "stuck" in school due to anxiety. Most students can benefit to some degree from better understanding their body's typical responses to unpredictable situations. The built-in strengths assessment is also an excellent way to help students with positive identity construction.

**IF . . . THEN**

If gaming technology is used to help develop self-regulation skills using strength-based techniques, and in so doing, generates physiological data on how the player's stress response changes with practice, then this can also be a strategy for **Output.**

OUTPUT

INPUT

 # Planner Options

**Offer many planner options.** The idea of using a planner to remember due dates, make lists, or display schedules is not new. Planners can be a very useful tool to input and remember information, but planner use is not intuitive or automatic for some students. Keeping a planner can be a cognitive challenge in itself before the student even gets to the homework. For a planner to be helpful, it needs to meet the needs of the user, not confuse the learner more. Here are a few alternatives to typical paper planners:

**Try This**

Pocket planner

- *Planner apps.* There are many apps available for smartphones and tablets. I am a big fan of IStudiez Pro for iPhones.

- *Homemade pocket planner.* The school planner did not work for my son, so I created a customized planner for him (pictured in the Try This section). The subjects in the planner are in the same order as his daily schedule. In middle school, when his daily schedule alternated, we alternated planner pages, too. It provides a space for study hall tasks and after-school tasks. There are even spaces to check when each task is done and handed in (all the stages of homework completion). Best of all, it fits in his pocket, relieving him of the energy it takes to keep track of yet another book.

- *Key chain tutor.* Kluth and Danaher (2010) shared the brilliant idea of a small tape recorder on a key chain that can be used to record reminders for students about homework, materials, or events.

## Why This Works

- **Research base.** The use of highly structured planning tools helps build organizational skills, time management, memory, and task completion skills (Kaufman, 2010).

- **Student involvement.** How useful a planner is can be very individualized. The same planner will not work for all students. Students should be involved in talking through what might work for them. Have them try different ones and decide which is best.

- **Reasonable use.** Paper planners, book or pocket size, are inexpensive (usually less than $10), as are small tape recorders for keychain tutors (less than $10). Apps range from free to $6.99, but the smartphones and tablets needed to run them are expensive.

*(continued)*

- **Expectations maintained.** Planners should be used to scaffold management skills without being used to penalize students if they do not use the planner as designed. Writing information in planners "correctly" should not be used as a homework assignment or incentive for rewards.

- **Equity and universality.** Schoolwide planners that are required of or provided to each student are not equitable. It is a little like expecting all the kids to wear the exact same style shoe. It might not be right for each one.

**IF . . . THEN**

If the right planner is used to support a student in completing tasks, then this can also be a strategy for **Output.**

OUTPUT

INPUT

# Web-Based Materials and Information

**Post materials and information on the web.**
One strategy that goes a long way in supporting many diverse needs is a class or teacher web site on which assignments, handouts, notes, announcements, web links, and any other helpful information is posted. There are many benefits.

- Those who use a lot of processing energy keeping track of handouts, taking notes, or recording assignments will not have to expend that energy. The information they need will be waiting for them whenever they can access the Internet.

- Students who recorded an assignment incorrectly but did not realize it until they opened the textbook at home have a way to self-check.

- Information posted and accessed on the computer can be adapted to visual and auditory needs more readily than hardcopy notes or handouts.

- It saves trees.

 **Try This**

Here is a list of web sites for posting materials:

**Blackboard**
http://www.blackboard.com

**TeacherEase**
http://www.teacherease.com

**Think Wave**
http://www.ThinkWave.com

## Why This Works

- **Research base.** This follows the principles of universal design (CAST, 2012).

- **Student involvement.** Offer options for students to post to the web site as well—blogs, chats, photo sharing. Tech savvy students can even help you keep your web site updated or at least remind you when it needs updating. Another classroom job: Web Master!

- **Reasonable use.** It does take time to learn how to set up a web site and keep it updated. With practice, it will be easier and faster to post materials and assignments than it is to print them or write them on the board!

- **Expectations maintained.** Posting materials provides students with what they need and teaches them how to use another resource. It supports them in being less dependent on teachers.

*(continued)*

- **Equity and universality.** Having a class web site helps level the playing field in many ways for students. For those who easily remember assignments and keep track of materials, the web site can be a place to post on a blog about the day's lesson. For students who struggle with remembering assignments and keeping track of materials, it provides them with an opportunity to use their energy and processing load for other things.

> **→ IF . . . THEN ←**
>
> If web sites are used to allow submission of homework by e-mail as another way to level the playing field, because performance will be based on work not on ability to keep track of the completed work-sheet, then this can also be a strategy for **Output.**
>
> OUTPUT
>
>

#  Graphic Organizers

**Offer a variety of graphic organizers.** A graphic organizer is any visual structure or symbol that is used to represent knowledge or concepts and any relationships among them. There are many forms of graphic organizers, such as Venn diagrams, concept maps, KWL charts, Ishikawa (fishbone) diagrams, webs, flow charts, mind maps, and storyboards. Graphic organizers promote patterning and construction of meaningful connections to previous learning. This goes beyond rote memorization to higher processing and application of information in significant ways.

##  Try This

Mind maps are a particularly effective type of graphic organizer:

**Mind Tools**

http://www.mindtools.com/index.html

**Mind Tools article about Mind Maps**

http://www.mindtools.com/pages/article/newISS_01.htm

One of the most fun and elaborate illustrated mind maps I have seen is Changing Education Paradigms by Sir Ken Robinson (http://comment.rsablogs.org.uk/2010/10/14/rsa-animate-changing-education-paradigms).

##  Why This Works

- **Research base.** "Graphic organizers help students see relationships and pattern new information for memory storage. They are one of the most nourishing of all 'dendrite sprout foods' to nurture students' brain growth" (Willis, 2006, p. 16).

- **Student involvement.** Students can take their notes using teacher-made graphic organizers or they can make their own. Any visual that depicts the knowledge to be learned is useful. Students can also rate the graphic organizers according to how helpful they are for various topics.

- **Reasonable use.** A graphic organizer is one of the cheapest, easiest things to use. There are several web sites with printable organizers:

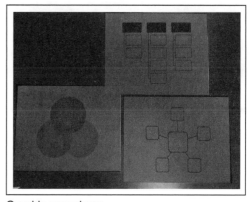
Graphic organizers

EdHelper.com: http://edhelper.com/teachers/graphic_organizers.htm

Education Oasis: http://www.educationoasis.com/curriculum/graphic_organizers.htm

Holt Interactive Graphic Organizers: http://my.hrw.com/nsmedia/intgos/html/igo.htm

TeacherVision: http://www.teachervision.fen.com/graphic-organizers/printable/6293.html

Thinkport: http://www.thinkport.org/technology/template.tp

*(continued)*

Input Through Executive Functions: Graphic Organizers

- **Expectations maintained.** Students are still accountable for knowing the big idea and the important details. Graphic organizers facilitate more complex learning, rather than simplifying the concepts.

- **Equity and universality.** Each student should have a choice of several readily available forms to use when/if wanted.

→ IF . . . THEN ←

If graphic organizers are used to help students organize and communicate their ideas more effectively, then this can also be a strategy for **Output.**

OUTPUT

# ·☐· Timers

**Use timers to support task completion.** "If we don't have an internal clock, sometimes we need an external one." This is the explanation a first-grade teacher gave to a student when he asked why a classmate had a timer on his desk during seatwork time. It really is as simple as that. Some of us have internal timers that help us to efficiently regulate and manage time and task completion. Some of us need to use external clocks instead. Online timers (analog or digital format) can be displayed for the whole class or used by individual students on individual computers or devices.

**Try This**

Timers

## Why This Works

- **Research base.** Time management is a higher order executive functioning skill. The components involved include making a schedule, planning, organizing, estimating task complexity and completion timing, and monitoring progress (Dawson & Guare, 2004). Limitations in temporal abilities have a negative impact on project and task completion (Kaufman, 2010).

- **Student involvement.** Have students try different timers or experiment with the placement of the timer, and poll the class about their preferences.

- **Reasonable use.** Online timers are free. Individual timers range in price. A favorite of mine is the Time Timer ($35.99).

- **Expectations maintained.** It is important to separate the student's ability to complete the task at hand (e.g., solving math problems, writing a paper, play a game) and the student's ability to manage time. Students should be evaluated on the work they produce, not the efficiency of completion. Scaffold students toward stronger time management skills. Understand that these skills must be taught and may not be internalized by some students.

- **Equity and universality.** I asked a class of college students if they liked to have a timer running during small-group activities or tests. "Does it help you manage your time better?" The responses were split pretty evenly into three groups: 1) Yes! It helps me monitor myself so I do not run out of time; 2) No! It just makes me more nervous, and I pay more attention to the timer than the task; and 3) I do not care—either way is fine. So, I asked, "How do I meet all of your needs then? Do I display the timer for group one and risk making group two nervous?

*(continued)*

Do I forgo the timer to meet group two's needs, while missing a chance to support group one?" Their suggestions were as follows:

Do not put a timer in front of the class. Those who need one can use their phones.

Put a timer in the middle of the classroom, facing one half of the class, and let students choose which side they sit on.

Display a timer in a discrete area so that it is available to those who like it but not distracting to others.

This is a great example of problem solving with students for equity and universality.

**→ IF . . . THEN ←**

If timers are used as supports during testing situations to facilitate evaluation of students on their academic abilities, not executive functioning abilities, then this can also be a strategy for **Assessment.**

ASSESSMENT

# Resource Ring

**Provide a resource ring for important information.** There is a lot of information to remember as an independent functioning adult—phone numbers for family, friends, and support agencies; addresses for community buildings, agencies, and businesses; schedules; grocery lists; special diet restrictions; recreation options; and more. If they cannot remember all of their resource options, young adults may end up relying too heavily on one person (e.g., mom, a counselor, a friend). A resource ring puts all of the information in one place so that students can refer to it quickly. It consists of several small cards on a key ring or karabiner clip so that students can fit it in a pocket or bag. The cards can be color coded: family members' phone numbers are in one color, frequently attended businesses are in another color, and so forth. Photos, icons, or braille can be added to help identify each resource.

**Try This**

Resource ring

## Why This Works

- **Research base.** Kluth and Danaher (2010) discussed the benefits of pocket cards for building study skills. A resource ring works the same way to support transition to adulthood.

- **Student involvement.** Students should compile their own resource ring so that it is personalized and organized the way they can best use it.

- **Reasonable use.** This item is very simple and cheap to implement. All you need is a ring or clip, colored cardstock, and a hole-punch.

- **Expectations maintained.** Creating and using a resource ring increases the level of independence for young adults. They should be expected to use multiple resources and have a place to check for information on their own before calling a parent, teacher, or friend.

- **Equity and universality.** Everyone needs a bank of information to refer to on occasion. This is another format for obtaining access to information.

> **→ IF . . . THEN ←**
>
> If a resource ring is used as a prompt for using resources and being independent, then this can also be a strategy for **Output.**
>
> OUTPUT
>
>

---

# A-to-C Chart

**Display scaffold of skills to show level of independence.** When my son was young, his very favorite thing in the whole world was watching TV. If he had his druthers, he would watch all day. Although enjoyable, watching TV was mentally exhausting for him. The way that he processed the stimuli left him irritable and unfocused in a short amount of time. It was difficult for him to understand why we limited TV time, his very favorite pastime. He wanted to know how old he had to be to make his own TV rules.

Knowing he needed a concrete visual to understand a complex answer, we used an A-to-C chart. A is for *adult* and C is for *child.* This visual shows how the adult first has all of the knowledge and skills. Step by

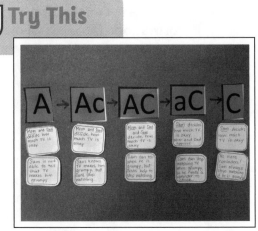

A-to-C chart

step, the adult scaffolds the child in building knowledge, skill, and independence until the child is independent. Each person is unique in the rate at which he or she goes through each step and the amount of direct instruction and supports needed along the way. The A-to-C chart is a powerful planning tool for purposefully supporting students through complex skills. Over the years, we have used this tool to assess my son's level of independence and need for supports in many different areas.

## Why This Works

- **Research base.** Vygotsky (1978) theorized that children construct knowledge and new learning by being scaffolded by more knowledgeable individuals. The A-to-C chart is one way to provide this scaffolding. Reciprocal teaching strategies like this have been advanced by Palincsar and Brown (1984).

- **Student involvement.** Students should be involved in this process by determining the letters to be used to represent themselves and the more knowledgeable individual, helping to determine how many steps there will be and what each will look like, and reflecting on how they are progressing toward independence.

- **Reasonable use.** This strategy requires some one-on-one time with the student to discuss each step and perhaps adapt the chart so the student can access it.

- **Expectations maintained.** This strategy facilitates high expectations because it provides a structure for planning steps toward a larger goal. Because the student knows that several steps may be needed until he or she is independent, the supports can be put in place incrementally over time.

- **Equity and universality.** An A-to-C chart can be customized for any academic, social, emotional, behavioral, physical, or linguistic goal. Symbols, photos, or written descriptions can be used at each step.

**→ IF . . . THEN ←**

If an A-to-C chart is used to help a student lay out a plan for self-evaluation at each step, then this can also be a strategy for **Assessment.**

ASSESSMENT

# Visual Goal Plan

**Use a storyboard to show students the transition process.** Making the transition from school to adult life is an abstract concept. It is difficult to picture what the transition will be like because the experiences are all new. Unlike transitions from grade level to grade level or even school to school, everything changes at once—new settings, new people, new routines, new expectations. The written IEP should include all of the details about the transition, but these still may be difficult for some students to understand. A storyboard can show all of the steps involved, including the timeline and people involved. Dialog or captioning might read like a social story to present accurate information and possible variations in a matter-of-fact way. In addition, some students may need to physically visit new settings and meet new people, taking photos while they are there. Including the photos in the storyboard will create a goal plan that is comfortable and comprehendible, not overwhelming or confusing.

 **Try This**

Transition storyboard

## Why This Works

- **Research base.** Using transitional storyboards is supported by Piaget's (1952) theory of cognitive development from concrete to abstract thinking.

- **Student involvement.** Students should be involved every step of the way as the storyboard is put together. Create a layout or structure ahead of time, but each time a piece is planned, the student helps put it into place in the story and create the dialog or caption for it.

- **Reasonable use.** Visits to new places and meetings to introduce new people may be time consuming, but there is no cost. Creating a storyboard entails visual materials and printing photos. It takes time, which is another incentive to start the planning process early!

- **Expectations maintained.** Students must be a part of their transition process. Any planning that takes place without the student is not in his or her best interest. It is not appropriate to make plans for other adults without their input.

- **Equity and universality.** Everyone has the right to feel comfortable and be fully informed and involved in his or her adult planning. All students in the class can develop and share storyboards of their future plans.

 IF . . . THEN

If storyboards, photos, or collages are used to help students express their own goals, then this can also be a strategy for **Output.**

OUTPUT

# Strategies for Output...

# PROVIDING MULTIPLE MEANS OF OUTPUT

Your students are engaged in learning, and you have provided multiple ways for them to obtain access to, perceive, process, and comprehend new information. The next step is to find out what they know and can do. In order to do this, students must have ways to express their knowledge, skills, and ideas.

The next principle of UDL is providing multiple means of action and expression or "output"—ways for students to show what they know. The two most common ways that students are expected to demonstrate their knowledge in school are through writing (e.g., tests, worksheets, essays) and oral responses to teacher-posed questions in class. Although these methods should be continued for the students who are able to demonstrate their learning in these ways, many more options need to be offered as well. Multiple means of expression include options for physical expression, options for communication, and options for executive functions (i.e., the functions of organization, planning, and task execution).

## Options for Physical Expression

Some students need to express themselves physically. They need to use their bodies beyond writing and speaking to show what they have learned. Maybe it means tracing letters or words in sand or shaving cream. Maybe it means operating a computer with a joystick, balance board, or eye controls rather than with a traditional mouse. It may mean acting out a concept instead of explaining it. The use of hands-on manipulatives, field trips outside of the classroom or school building, and movement around the classroom is essential. Providing options for physical expression also means making sure that everything in the classroom is physically accessible to all students and teachers.

## Options for Communication

Not all students are able to express themselves and their knowledge through traditional writing and speaking. It is important to offer many different ways for students to communicate with an audience. Some alternatives for communication include drawing, creating storyboards, film design, music composition, model making, and sculpture. Assistive technology to help with the writing process may include speech-to-text software, spellcheckers, word-prediction software, and social media such as online discussion forums and blogs.

## Options for Executive Functions

Your executive functions are essentially the chief directors of your brain. Another apt metaphor is that they are the maestro who conducts your orchestra of skills and abilities (Packer, 2010). Executive functions help you decide when and how to use each skill that you have. They are the managers—time managers, material managers, goal setters, planners, task initiators, attention sustainers, and social skill regulators. Everyone has executive functions, but some people have stronger ones than others.

According to the National Center on Universal Design for Learning (2011), executive abilities are reduced when executive functioning capacity must be devoted to managing lower level skills and responses that are not automatic or fluent, thus the capacity for higher level functions is used up, and executive capacity is reduced due to disability or to lack of fluency with executive strategies.

UDL responds to stresses on executive functioning by scaffolding lower level skills (e.g., keeping track of time and materials) so that they become more automatic. Once lower level skills are more automatic, higher level executive skills (e.g., long-term goal setting; managing a multistep, complex project) can become more developed (National Center on Universal Design for Learning, 2011). Skills to be scaffolded include goal setting, planning, developing strategies that work best for various tasks, managing information to make sense of it, managing all the resources available, and self-monitoring progress. Scaffolding does not mean doing the work for the students. It means providing a boost or support so that the students can accomplish the work themselves. Then, the support is gradually withdrawn or reduced on an individual basis until the student is as independent as possible.

## CONSIDERATIONS

There are several considerations to keep in mind when providing multiple ways for students to demonstrate their understanding.

### Providing Multiple Means of Expression Is Not the Same as "Any Student Performance Will Do"

As with the other UDL principles, expectations are not lowered in any way when offering various means of expression, or output. Rather, high expectations are maintained for all students. Multiple, varied, responsive opportunities are provided for students to demonstrate their understanding of concepts, development of knowledge, and mastery of skills in divergent, creative ways. Simply put, there is not just one way to show what you know.

### Changing Our Idea of What It Means to Be Successful in School

Most teachers would agree that there are many ways to show what you know. Many of those teachers, though, would say that multiple means of output are valuable, but in the end, students still need to know how to read, write, and speak to be successful in school and to be prepared for the next grade, the next school, and a career.

Consider this experience: By the start of middle school, Tyler had a difficult time writing lengthy text responses to comprehension questions. However, he could create elaborate drawings with minute detail and highly descriptive dialog in speech bubbles that clearly demonstrated his intricate understanding of any content that he read or heard. Some teachers allowed the drawing as an exception but required him to write a vast majority of the time. Other teachers did not allow the drawing at all. Tyler spent so much time and energy on the effort of writing text that his responses were brief, oversimplified, or incomplete, depriving teachers from seeing how much he really knew. Tyler could often be heard asking if he had to do it "the school way" or if he could do it "his way." He clearly saw a mismatch between school expectations and his abilities. They did not fit. It was not long before he saw himself as a mismatch, a misfit. By the end of middle school, this bright, capable, talented young man described himself as "dumb" and "bad at school."

Tyler certainly was not dumb, but he was unsuccessful at school. The tighter we cling to the school way of expressing knowledge and skills, the more students we are excluding. Inclusion does not mean that everyone responds in the same way or creates the same products. Inclusion means everyone responding in ways that they can to participate fully in meaning-making activities in the learning environment. For some, the best way is writing text or speaking. For others, it is drawing or pointing or typing or demonstrating. For some, it is papers and tests. For others, it is projects or presentations or art.

All students should be encouraged to build their skills in many different ways. If writing is possible, then writing skills should be taught and developed as much as possible. In the meantime, if there is another way that allows students to show how much more they know, they should not be deprived of that option. The more means of expression that students develop, the more versatile they will be in various settings at various tasks. If we only teach them one way, they will only be able to do it one way. It does students a disservice to limit their response skills. We need to broaden the options until there is no distinction between the school way and the student's way. The school way needs to be every way.

## How It All Comes Together

The foundational theories reinforce this principle of UDL as well. Tomlinson and McTighe (2006) agreed that students differ in the ways they best show what they have learned. They emphasized that evidence of student understanding is revealed when students apply or transfer knowledge in authentic contexts, and teachers, students, and districts benefit by "working smarter" (p. 9) and using technology and other means to collaboratively design, share, and critique units of study.

There are three important issues wrapped up in these beliefs. First, students show they truly understand a concept through six facets of understanding: They can explain, interpret, apply, have perspective, display empathy, and have self-knowledge. Second, students must have authentic contexts to show their understanding through these facets. Examples of inauthentic work include fill-in-the-blank exercises, selecting answers from given choices, solving contrived problems, practicing decontextualized skills, or diagramming sentences. Authentic work includes conducting research or experiments, debating a controversial issue, or interpreting literature. Third, students must have choice in which authentic tasks they do.

Gay (2010) asserted that school communication may not match students' communication styles or abilities. Without a shared frame of reference, miscommunication occurs. There is not one right way or one wrong way to communicate, but some ways that students communicate are seen as nonstandard in a given situation. When this happens, the student may be seen as less knowledgeable or skillful because the message was not received as intended.

Willis (2006) contended that in order for students to be successful out of school, they need to have skills that computers or robots do not have. These include expert thinking (recognizing and organizing patterns and identifying and solving new problems as they arise) and complex communications (careful listening, observing to interpret and convey critical information). These skills go beyond rote learning and standardized tasks.

Kliewer (1998) deeply challenged the school way of participating of days past. Inclusion in the community means that you have the opportunity to participate in that community and be valued as a full citizen. If there is no one right way to participate and if multiple ways of participating are encouraged and provided, then everyone in the community is included and valued. Kliewer (1998) has gone on to say that incompetence does not reside in a child, but it is ascribed to a child by those who misunderstand the meaning of the child's participation. Miscommunication similarly does not reside in a particular individual. It resides between individuals, in the web where communication is shared and evolves. So, the label "communication disordered" is not valid. One person does not have a problem or a disorder. The problem occurs in between the two people because there is a mismatch between the way a message is sent and the way it is received. If we provide many different ways to send and receive information and ideas, there are more matches. Finally, Kliewer (1998) addressed the idea of "socially imposed illiteracy" (p. 98). Students are only illiterate if society does not recognize their ways of being literate. If we expand how we define *literate*, all students can actively participate in the construction of meaning, realizing all literate capabilities.

# ·⌐▯⌐· Mobility Supports

**Provide many supports for mobility and orientation.** A fully inclusive classroom is one where everyone feels safe and at home and where everyone can move about freely, efficiently, and comfortably. For students with mobility needs, whether they have a visual impairment or perhaps use a wheelchair, walker, cane, or crutches, the classroom should be set up and include strategies such as the following to support mobility and orientation:

Mobility supports

- Wide aisles

- Uncluttered work spaces

- Adjustable height and tilt tables or desks

- All equipment and supplies within reach

- All furniture, storage spaces, equipment labeled with tactile labels

- Ergonomic backpacks to keep hands free

Think about what makes sense to keep everyone safe, versus trying to create a perfect, artificial environment.

Here are a few web sites to visit:

- Perkins School for the Blind: http://www.perkins.org

- Texas School for the Blind and Visually Impaired: http://www.tsbvi.edu

- Texas School for the Blind and Visually Impaired's Environmental Checklist for Developing Independence: http://www.tsbvi.edu/orientation-a-mobility/1969-environmental-checklist-for-developing-independence

 ## Why This Works

- **Research base.** "A rich physical environment versus a restricted environment and encouragement to engage the environment rather than being protected from it positively affects development" (Brown, 2010, p. 1).

- **Student involvement.** Everyone should be a part of maintaining a safe classroom and including everyone in activities. This means teaching all students to clean up after themselves, introduce themselves when they enter a group or conversation, indicate when they are leaving, and not be too overprotective, for example.

Output Through Space: Mobility Supports

- **Reasonable use.** This does not entail adding equipment to the classroom. Rather, it means thinking about how the room is arranged and maintained.

- **Expectations maintained.** Teaching means finding ways for all students to become more independent rather than having other people do things for them or make things easier for them. They will learn more if they have to figure things out for themselves.

- **Equity and universality.** It is everyone's classroom. Everyone in the room should be able to get to a place or use supplies.

> → IF . . . THEN ←
>
> If mobility supports are used to create a safe, comfortable, and enriching place that encourages independence, then this can also be a strategy for **Engagement.**
>
> ENGAGEMENT
>
>

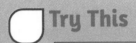

# Student-Created Bulletin Boards

**Encourage student-created bulletin boards.** Have students express what they know about a topic or concept by displaying it on a bulletin board. This can be done individually, in small groups, or as a whole class. Be sure to teach them the benefit of having a dark border to reduce visual overstimulation!

**Try This**

Student-created bulletin board

## Why This Works

- **Research base.** Providing students with the opportunity to show their uniqueness and creativity establishes a sense of belonging in the classroom community (Nelson et al., 2000).

- **Student involvement.** Let students decide for themselves if they want to post their classwork on the board. If they do, encourage them to decide which is their best or favorite work. This will encourage them to reflect on their accomplishments rather than wait to see what you consider to be the most valuable.

- **Reasonable use.** Supplies for bulletin boards are inexpensive. There is no need to purchase commercial borders or fancy lettering. The more the students create, the more they express themselves.

- **Expectations maintained.** This is another way to express knowledge. Once students are finished, you can ask them questions about their ideas or about details you do not see represented. They can then decide if they want to modify the display.

- **Equity and universality.** Everyone should have the opportunity to participate in creating bulletin boards and to work with different students each time. Provide supports for each step of the process—planning and execution.

> **▶ IF . . . THEN ◀**
>
> If student-created bulletin boards are used so that a teacher can evaluate knowledge and skills, then this can also be a strategy for **Assessment.**
>
> ASSESSMENT

# Coded Assignments

**Code and cue assignments.** Coding an assignment can help students focus on a particular part of the assignment or avoid another part so that their attention and stamina is spent working on the skill at hand. Here are some ideas for coding assignments:

- Highlight in yellow the questions to answer first.

- Paperclip the page to start on.

- Put a sticker of a hand on a homework paper or specific questions that they can get "a helping hand" with; no hand means they should do it independently.

- Number textbooks, folders, or supplies to show the order in which to use them.

- Color code math problems to highlight different operations (Kluth & Danaher, 2010).

- Use little arrow sticky notes to draw attention to instructions.

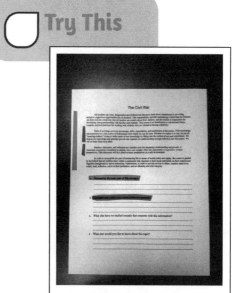

**Try This**

Coded assignment

## Why This Works

- **Research base.** Make sure you determine the best supports for your students' ability, interest, and age. You want to use a cue that helps them be more independent on the academic skill rather than a cue that is distracting or does too much for them (Cohen & Sloan, 2007).

- **Student involvement.** The coding can gradually be handed over to the student. Provide students with a pack of arrow sticky notes and instruct them to place the notes on instructions that they want to review again at home before starting the work.

- **Reasonable use.** The only materials entailed are typical office supplies—highlighters, markers, sticky notes, paper clips, stickers. The most difficult part is determining the most needed supports for different students.

- **Expectations maintained.** The codes or cues do not complete the task for the student. Rather, they direct students' attention where it is needed so that they can be more independent and work more efficiently.

- **Equity and universality.** Introduce codes and cues to all students in the classroom so that they have the choice of whether or not to use them.

▶ IF . . . THEN ◀

If coded assignments are used to sort and present information to facilitate processing of new concepts, then this can also be a strategy for **Input.**

INPUT

# Supports for Interactive Whiteboards

**Provide supports for access to the interactive whiteboard.** The interactive whiteboard is an amazing tool, but the tools may be difficult to physically maneuver or the areas of the board difficult to reach. Students may be reluctant to come to the board and use it in front of others. Here are two alternatives to using the whiteboard stylus tools or a finger:

- *Extended pointers:* Smart Moves (http://www .smartmovespointer.com) and Learning Resources (http://www.learningresources.com) make long-handled pointers that can reach any part of the whiteboard.

- *Switches and switch adapters:* These are large buttons that can be used to click on the desired area of the whiteboard without physically touching it (like a mouse). They can be connected with a wire or wirelessly. (Find instructions at http://www .youtube.com/watch?v=oFhs-hDLE3E.)

Pointer used for Grade 1

Pointer used for Grade 11

## Why This Works

- **Research base.** Gross motor interaction with this technology is the precursor for fine motor skill development (Clark & Nordness, 2007).

- **Student involvement.** Students can be scaffolded in their participation as they feel comfortable approaching the board and using the different tools. Involve students in the installation of the switch so that they can see how the technology works and practice following video instructions.

- **Reasonable use.** Interactive whiteboards are expensive ($600–$2,000), but adapted tools are relatively inexpensive ($10 for a set of pointers or about $50 for a switch).

- **Expectations maintained.** These adaptations provide a way to gain access to technology and express learning. Students learn the academic content as well as technology skills.

- **Equity and universality.** The interactive whiteboard is only a support for inclusion if everyone has the same opportunity to use it.

→ IF . . . THEN ←

If supports for interactive whiteboards are used to motivate interaction with this effective teaching tool, then this can also be a strategy for **Engagement.**

ENGAGEMENT

# Writing Supports

**Provide fine-motor and gross-motor supports for writing.** When developing writing skills, as appropriate, students may need fine- and gross-motor supports for the physical act of writing. Here are several examples:

 **Try This**

- *Pencil grips:* There are several different kinds of pencil grips that guide students' fingers to the correct grasp or help build arch support. They also make the pencil easier to hold with less hand strength. Customized grips can be made with playdough or hardening foam.

- *Pencil weights:* Similar to grips, these slide on the pencil to weigh it down so less pressure is needed by the user to write.

Writing supports

- *Twist 'N Write pencil:* Shaped like a wishbone, this pen is designed for maximum control and minimum stress on the hand.

- *Wrist straps:* These connect the wrist and the pencil with two loops for better control and maximum feedback regarding pencil movement.

- *Highlighted or raised-line paper:* Paper with every other line shaded or highlighted, as well as paper with every line raised helps guide a student to stay on the line while writing.

- *Different writing utensils:* Markers, crayons, or gel pens require less pressure.

- *Desktop easels or writing boards:* These provide an inclined writing surface anywhere the student needs it.

- *Paper stabilizers:* These weigh or clamp the paper down so it does not move about while writing.

These web sites offer several products:

- School Specialty: http://www.schoolspecialty.com

- Therapy Shoppe: http://www.therapyshoppe.com

- Therapy Fun Zone: http://therapyfunzone.com/blog/ot/fine-motor-skills

## Why This Works

- **Research base.** Fine-motor control includes weight bearing on the hands, postural control, shoulder stability, development of the arches of the hand and the thumb, in-hand manipulation, bilateral integration, and hand strength (Cooley, 2013).

- **Student involvement.** Introduce a fine-motor skill need to students and involve them in brainstorming a solution for support. You might say, "Even with a pencil grip, the crayons in our classroom are too short for some of us to use effectively. Any ideas?" As students make suggestions, steer them toward solutions that do not rely on friends or classmates using the crayons for each other. Emphasize strategies that help everyone do it alone.

- **Reasonable use.** Homemade writing supports are nearly free, especially if you gather supplies at the dollar store. You can highlight your own paper or glue a large binder clip to a wide three-ring notebook in lieu of a commercial desktop easel. Here are approximate prices for several different commercial writing supports:

  *Pencil grips:* $2–$5

  *Pencil weights:* $40–$50 for a set of 3–4

  *Twist 'N Write pencil:* $2 (http://www.drawyourworld .com/twist-n-write/)

  *Wrist strap:* $8–$10

  *Highlighted or raised-line paper:* $15 for 100-sheet pack

  *Different writing utensils:* $3–$10 for a set of 10

  *Desktop easels or writing boards:* $50–$80

  *Paper stabilizers:* $4 each

- **Expectations maintained.** The purpose of writing is to convey thoughts and ideas to an audience through text or print. These supports facilitate this so that students become more independent in expressing themselves.

- **Equity and universality.** These supports are for students whose goals are to develop handwriting skills. Other students may use facilitated, augmented, or alternative communication instead. The purpose is that every student is supported when communicating thoughts and ideas to others.

> → IF . . . THEN ←
>
> If writing supports are used as test modifications rather than a scribe, and as long as they are effective enough in reducing fatigue and processing time so that a student is evaluated on knowledge rather than handwriting ability, then this can also be a strategy for **Assessment.**
>
> ASSESSMENT

# Universal Tools

**Ensure the environment can be used by all.** In addition to supporting mobility and orientation in the classroom, it is important to be sure that all equipment can be used by every student. Just about anything students might use in a classroom is available in a universally designed format: spring action scissors, easy slide staple remover, handled rules, low push-button light switches, lever handles on doors and faucets, click pens (no caps), large button talking calculators, push button padlocks, ramps, motion-sensor lights and doors, push-latch cabinets and drawers, automatic close drawers.

## Try This

Universal tools

Check out these ideas:

- The Center for Universal Design: http://www.ncsu.edu/ncsu/design/cud/index.htm

- Center for Inclusive Design and Environmental Access: http://idea.ap.buffalo.edu/

## Why This Works

- **Research base.** The principles of universal design are equitable use, flexibility in use, simple and intuitive use, perceptible information, tolerance for error, low physical effort, and size and shape for approach and use (North Carolina State University [NCSU], 1997).

- **Student involvement.** Students can be involved in solving problems as they arise. Encourage them to be inventors.

- **Reasonable use.** Depending on the product, cost and expertise needed to use it is variable; however, the less expensive and easier to use, the better designed it is.

- **Expectations maintained.** For all students, teaching means finding ways for them to become more independent rather than doing things for them or making things easier for them.

- **Equity and universality.** Products with universal design features make tasks easier for every user, accommodate a range of needs and abilities, adapt as needs change, are attractive and safe, and are not just for people with disabilities (Yearns, 2004).

> **→ IF . . . THEN ←**
>
> If universal tools are used so that students are able to interact with all parts of the classroom, then this can also be a strategy for **Engagement.**
>
> ENGAGEMENT

# Integrative Movement

**Include integrative movement in the daily schedule to enhance expression of ideas.**
Some examples of mind–body integrative movement are walking, dancing, skipping, twirling, Tai Chi, and yoga. Just a few minutes of integrative movement each day can help to increase student performance in several areas including reading, writing, test taking, physical tasks, and musical and artistic performance. Brain Gym, established in 1987 by the Educational Kinesiology Foundation, has been shown to have an impressive impact on reading and math performance (Hannaford, 2005). Brain Gym consists of a series of focused, physical movements that can be performed easily and quickly in any classroom space without equipment. Yoga provides students healthy ways to express and balance their emotions; eases anxiety and tension (e.g., pretest or performance jitters); and enhances focus, concentration, comprehension, memory, organizational skills, communication skills, motor skills, and balance.

Visit these web sites for more information and ideas:

- Brain Gym: http://www.braingym.org

- Yoga 4 Classrooms: http://www.yoga4classrooms.com

- Tai Chi for Kids: http://www.taichiforkids.com

## Try This

Brain gym

## Why This Works

- **Research base.** The body plays an integral part in cognitive processes. Movements express knowledge, facilitate cognitive function, and help develop nerve cell networks in the brain as they grow more complex (Hannaford, 2005).

- **Student involvement.** Students can follow the teacher's instructions or use integrative movements on their own when needed. Students can choose the movements to be used each day.

- **Reasonable use.** Brain Gym, Tai Chi, and yoga require training sessions, but dancing and walking do not. Until you are familiar with the more formal movements, it is simple and easy to take a couple minutes each day or class to walk, stretch, or march.

*(continued)*

- **Expectations maintained.** Students are still expected to express what they know and use their class time productively. Integrative movement provides a support to do just that.

- **Equity and universality.** All methods of integrative movement can be adapted for any physical need.

→ IF . . . THEN ←

If integrative movement is used before listening to lectures or studying material because the exercises facilitate better processing, then this can also be a strategy for **Input.**

INPUT

# Transition Areas

**Provide a transition waiting area in the classroom.** Transition times in the classroom (e.g., moving to and from special classes, dismissal time) can be difficult. The shift in focus and the change in expectations call for purposeful management strategies. Clear expectations and student self-management are two key elements for smooth transitions. Golden (2012) and Kluth and Danaher (2010) have all suggested the idea of marking or arranging a transition area. If you place markers on the floor (or chairs along the wall), spaced adequately apart, students can tell where to stand or sit while they wait at the door. If each student is on a marker, no students will bunch up or linger behind. Providing a transition area can also scaffold understanding of personal space.

At one primary school, there are masking tape lines along both sides of the floor in every hallway. They are off to the side, but still a few feet from the wall. When students are in the hallway, they focus on staying on the line. It keeps them from bunching up or touching items on display in the halls.

**Try This**

Transition areas

## Why This Works

- **Research base.** Wong and Wong (1998) listed these aspects of a well-managed classroom: Students are deeply involved with their work; students know what is expected of them; there is relatively little wasted time, confusion, or disruption; and the climate of the classroom is work-oriented but relaxed.

- **Student involvement.** A great idea for a class meeting is discussing ways to make transitions smoother and quicker. Ask students what is most difficult about transitions (e.g., switching gears from one task to another; coping with anxiety or excitement; knowing what to do, where to go, or what to bring) and brainstorm solutions.

- **Reasonable use.** Creating a transition area requires only masking tape or extra school chairs.

- **Expectations maintained.** This idea focuses student attention and supports them so that they can act independently during transition times.

*(continued)*

- **Equity and universality.** Providing a transition area gives all students what they need at these times. Remember to ensure that all students have a turn to be the Line Leader (or better yet, Trailblazer) if they choose.

> **→ IF . . . THEN ←**
>
> If transition areas are labeled by names or skill concepts (e.g., coins, letters, numbers) so that students can reinforce learning while lining up, then this can also be a strategy for **Input.**
>
> INPUT
>

# Coded Classroom

**Practice ways to code the classroom setting.**
Particularly in elementary school classrooms, but also at the middle and high school levels, there are many materials for each student—books, folders, cubbies or lockers, pencils, crayons or markers, furniture, and additional supplies. Some students may need support locating their own items and distinguishing them from others'. There are different ways to code each student's belongings so that they match each other and are easily identifiable to their owner (e.g., with color, text labels, photos, fabric swatches, stickers). You can even glue small objects on!

 **Try This**

**Must-read**

Golden, C. (2012). *The special educator's toolkit: Everything you need to organize, manage, and monitor your classroom.* Baltimore, MD: Paul H. Brookes Publishing Co.

Coded classroom

## Why This Works

- **Research base.** Coding the classroom is one way to teach students how to organize themselves for future success (Golden, 2012). This also relates to the continuum of abstractness if you pair concrete prompts (child's photo) with more abstract prompts (text label).

- **Student involvement.** Students should help decide how to code their materials. As labels wear out and need to be replaced, you can reflect with students about whether or not they are ready for a new format (e.g., "Do you still want/need your photo attached, or should we write your name?").

- **Reasonable use.** Coding the classroom will require some time in the beginning of the year to determine how each student's belongings should be coded and then accomplishing the task. It may mean purchasing a large set of permanent colored markers ($20) or stickers ($1–$3 per pack), for example. It also may mean gathering many small fabric remnants from the clearance bin at a fabric store or collecting small objects (e.g., Lego blocks, shells, beads).

- **Expectations maintained.** This strategy supports students in locating and using their own materials, increasing independence, and fostering executive functioning abilities.

- **Equity and universality.** Coding the classroom creates a sense of ownership for everyone.

→ IF . . . THEN ←

If the codes are used as a means to represent concepts in a new way, then this can also be a strategy for **Input.**

INPUT

# Photo Essay

**Encourage photography to express ideas.** Good practice following a school field trip or event is to have a discussion in the classroom about the experience and what was learned, or perhaps complete a guide sheet or other written assignment. For students who have difficulty remembering the details of the experience, have difficulty expressing those details, or have difficulty completing the written assignment, a photo essay of the event is an alternate way to share their perspective and new learning. The photos can show classmates and teachers what the student saw and did, and they can be used as prompts for the student to recall more details to share. The series of photos with captions can replace any written assignment.

## Try This

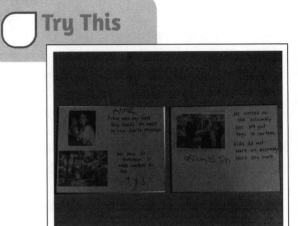

Photo essay

## Why This Works

- **Research base.** There is no means of expression that is suited to all learners. Providing multiple means of expression is essential for all students to be included in the learning environment (CAST, 2011).

- **Student involvement.** Students should use the camera themselves, with support if needed, so the photos are from their own perspective.

- **Reasonable use.** Cameras can be costly, but they do not have to be. Most cell phones have built in cameras, or one-time use cameras can be purchased from any drugstore.

- **Expectations maintained.** Students are still expected to participate in the activity, record and reflect on their experience, and contribute to the follow-up discussion.

- **Equity and universality.** The choice to do a photo essay instead of a written or oral presentation should be provided to all students. Expectations about how many photographs or captions can be differentiated individually.

> ➤ IF . . . THEN ◀
>
> If photo essays are used because the use of a camera is motivating and novel, then this can also be a strategy for **Engagement.**
>
> ENGAGEMENT
>
> 🔗

# Universal Computer Equipment

**Ensure that all computers are accessible.**
Computers can be a powerful teaching and learning tool if everyone has access to them. The following items of assistive technology can be used for computer hardware:

**Try This**

**Visit the AbleNet web site:**
http://www.ablenetinc.com/Assistive-Technology/Computer-Access

- *Adapted keyboards:* large button keyboards, color-coded keys, Braille keys, one-handed keyboards, alphabetic (versus QWERTY) layout, on-screen keyboards operated with a switch, and Freehand (an interactive glove!)

- *Mouse alternatives:* trackballs, joysticks, pointing devices, and switches, such as a head switch or a button switch

- *Monitor adaptations:* large monitors, antiglare screens, adjustable color contrasts

## Why This Works

- **Research base.** The principles of universal design are equitable use, flexibility in use, simple and intuitive use, perceptible information, tolerance for error, low physical effort, and size and shape for approach and use (NCSU, 1997).

- **Student involvement.** Teach students how each of the adaptations works and how it supports different needs. Have them reflect on whether they can accomplish that skill with or without the support of the assistive technology.

- **Reasonable use.** Computer hardware assistive technology is rather high-tech, so it is expensive. For example

  *Adapted keyboards:* $35–$150; Freehand: $250

  *Mouse alternatives:* $100–$400

  *Adapted monitors:* $200–$3,000; Antiglare screens: $50–$100

- **Expectations maintained.** Students are learning technological skills and multiple means for expressing their learning.

- **Equity and universality.** Ideally, all computers are universally designed so that they can be approached and used by everyone. If you have special stations for individual students, that is differentiation. It is equitable, but if everyone can use every station, that is universal design. Then, everyone has the same choice of stations.

**→ IF . . . THEN ←**

If universal computer equipment is used in testing or performance evaluations so that teachers can evaluate knowledge and skills separate from computer use, then this can also be a strategy for **Assessment.**

ASSESSMENT

# Communication Supports

**Provide augmentative and alternative communication (AAC) supports.** The area of AAC is vast, and this strategy page cannot do it justice. What it can do is provide definitions and some examples. AAC includes all forms of communication other than oral speech. Students who do not use oral speech effectively to express themselves use AAC. There are both unaided (making use of the student's body with signs, gestures, body language, facial expression) and aided communication systems (using low-tech to high-tech tools in addition to the student's body). Aided communication systems include

- **Low-tech**

  Symbol sets and systems such as Picture Communication Symbols (PCS), Blissymbols, or Widget Literacy Symbols

  Tangible symbols or objects of reference

- **High-tech**

  Eye gaze systems in which the individual uses his or her eyes to select words or phrases on the computer screen

  Text-to-speech systems in which the user types a message and it is spoken for him or her

  Voice output communication aids (VOCAs) in which the user manually or electronically chooses a preprogrammed word or phrase

## Try This

**American Speech-Language-Hearing Association**

http://www.asha.org/public/speech/disorders/AAC/

**Picture Communication Symbols**

http://www.mayer-johnson.com/category/symbols-and-photos

Communication supports

## Why This Works

- **Research base.** Use of AAC may increase social interaction, school performance, and feelings of self-worth (American Speech-Language-Hearing Association [ASHA], 2013).

- **Student involvement.** Share a quote with students and have them reflect on what it means. For younger students, try this quote from a poster by Scope (http://www.scope.org.uk): "Just because I couldn't speak, they thought I had nothing to say." For older students, try this quote by Norman Kunc: "Inclusion without communication is benevolence" (Kunc, 2013).

- **Reasonable use.** Low-tech systems are more reasonable than high-tech systems, but they are all fairly expensive. A set of Picture Communication Symbols is about $150. Addendum sets for particular topics are $20–$100. High-tech devices are $5,000–$10,000, but Medicare may pay the majority of the cost. Significant training is involved with high-tech devices.

- **Expectations maintained.** AAC users should not stop using speech if they are able to do so. AAC aids and devices are used to enhance their communication (ASHA, 2013).

- **Equity and universality.** Communication systems are highly individualized, set-up and programmed for a specific user. These aids will not be used by everyone in the class, but expressive communication will.

▶ IF . . . THEN ◀

If AAC is used to facilitate social inter-action, then this can also be a strategy for **Engagement.**

ENGAGEMENT

# Graph Paper

**Use graph paper to structure written responses.** For students who have difficulty with handwriting or visual-spatial processing, graph paper is a simple, effective support. Here are ways teachers have used graph papers:

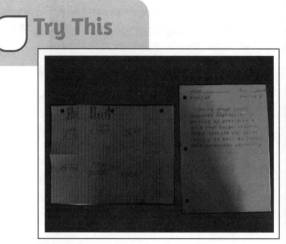

Graph paper

- **Math**

  Keep rows and columns organized when working number problems

  Trace the boxes in groups to use as arrays

  Trace the boxes individually to use in lieu of manipulatives

  Use for all written work in case a figure or graph is needed

- **Writing**

  Reminds students to leave one space between words

  Allows students to create margins, columns, or wrap text around figures

- **Study skills in all areas**

  Facilitates cuing assignments by drawing a box around certain features

  Facilitates highlighting, connecting ideas with arrows, and drawing graphic organizers

When graph paper is not available to use for math problems, ruled notebook paper can be turned sideways to create columns, or one page placed sideways under another creates a makeshift graph.

## Why This Works

- **Research base.** Dysgraphia is a learning disability that affects writing. Because writing requires a complex set of motor and information processing skills, dysgraphia can lead to problems with spelling; handwriting; putting thoughts on paper; and organizing letters, numbers, and words on a line (National Center for Learning Disabilities, 2012).

- **Student involvement.** Students can use graph paper for any written work. Make sure it is available at all times, along with notebook paper.

- **Reasonable use.** Graph paper is a little more expensive than ruled filler paper, particularly in a spiral or bound book, but it is still a very cost-effective strategy given all of its uses.

- **Expectations maintained.** This is a support to facilitate greater independence for students' written work.

- **Equity and universality.** The only argument I have ever heard against the use of graph paper is that students who frequently use graph paper will have more difficulty switching to lined filler paper. Why can't they always use graph paper? Even when it is not available, a sheet of lined paper turned sideways under another has the same effect.

→ IF . . . THEN ←

If graph paper is used to create graphic organizers or other visuals when notetaking, then this can also be a strategy for **Engagement.**

ENGAGEMENT

# Socratic Seminars

**Add Socratic seminars to lessons.** Socratic seminars are discussion-based instructional methods that entail students reading a selected text, formulating their own questions about the reading, then discussing each other's questions in a large group—sitting in a circle so that all members of the discussion are positioned equally for participation. Most of the discussion is based on prepared questions, but there is always time at the end for open discussion and reflection. Teachers act as facilitators and do not chime in their thoughts until the open reflection. Students are encouraged to disagree with each other and are guided in respectful disagreements that further critical thinking about the text. Socratic seminars can be used at any age. (You can find several videos of Socratic seminars at all age levels on YouTube [http://www.youtube.com].)

## Try This

Socratic seminars

## Why This Works

- **Research base.** Chorzempa and Lapidus (2009) reported that using Socratic seminars in inclusive classes has many benefits for all students, including encouraging complex thinking skills, analyzing text, exploring elements of a story, preparing written responses, developing responsibility, fostering independence, focusing thoughts, and building community.

- **Student involvement.** Socratic seminars are facilitated by teachers, but the students are the ones teaching each other and constructing meaning and responses together throughout the discussion.

- **Reasonable use.** Planning and practice is necessary for a successful seminar, but there is no cost associated with holding a seminar.

- **Expectations maintained.** Expectations for the content are maintained, and expectations for engagement with peers is increased.

- **Equity and universality.** Socratic seminars are culturally responsive in that they offer a way for students to express multiple perspectives in a safe, encouraging atmosphere. Difficult topics and disagreements are facilitated respectfully.

> **→ IF . . . THEN ←**
>
> If Socratic seminars are used to encourage discussion among students with multiple viewpoints and build a rich learning community, then this can also be a strategy for **Engagement.**
>
> ENGAGEMENT
>
>

# Student Recordings and Videos

**Allow students to record and videotape responses.** Just as tape-recorded lectures or reminders, books on tape, and teacher-made videos can help students input information, recordings and videos can help students express their learning. Sometimes students are better able to talk through what they know about a particular topic than they are able to write about it. By creating a skit or commercial, for example, students can use drama as a means of output.

Student videos

A middle school social studies teacher assigned a choice of projects for a unit on the Revolutionary War. Students could choose to prepare a paper, an oral report, or any other project with teacher approval. Three middle school students chose to create a video about a specific part of the Revolutionary War. They wrote scripts (adding several elements of humor), created costumes, and filmed several scenes. They expressed the important details so well with such meaningful connections that the teacher continues to use the video each year as an exemplary expression of the content.

## Why This Works

- **Research base.** Drama can be an effective way to practice and develop communication skills (Chatterton & Butler, 1994).

- **Student involvement.** Students can be involved in adapting assignment requirements or rubrics to include recording oral responses or videotaping dramatic responses.

- **Reasonable use.** It may take more time for the teacher to evaluate student responses.

- **Expectations maintained.** Responses must be made completely by the student, just as they would be in writing, and they must contain the same details and expression of knowledge and skills. Be sure that the effort students put into scripts, costumes, and filming is not confused with how much they understand the concept they are to be demonstrating.

- **Equity and universality.** In order for students to have the choice to record responses or record dramatic representations of concepts, they need to have access to the necessary

*(continued)*

equipment. If they do not have the equipment at home, time can be provided in school, or they can borrow the necessary equipment. Lack of equipment at home should not preclude a student from being able to choose this option for an assignment.

**IF . . . THEN**

If student recordings and videos are used as an alternative summative evaluation or home-work option, then this can also be a strategy for **Assessment.**

ASSESSMENT

# Prequestions

**Provide students with discussion questions before the lesson.** Large-group discussion may be difficult or anxiety-provoking for some students. If they have a difficult time processing what is being said by everyone, or they are nervous about being called on, they will not be able to respond to any of the discussion questions, even if they understand the content. On her web site (http://www.paulakluth.com), Paula Kluth shares a simple, effective tip: Provide students with the discussion questions that will be asked before the lesson. This gives students time to formulate a response and think through a point that they want to make. When it is their turn in a discussion, they will be better prepared or they can read from a premade cue card.

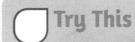 Try This

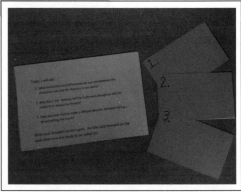

Prequestions

## Why This Works

- **Research base.** Strategies such as the one depicted in the photo, are devoted to promoting inclusive schooling and positive ways of supporting students with autism and other disabilities.

- **Student involvement.** Students can ask for the discussion questions or retrieve them ahead of time if posted on a class web site.

- **Reasonable use.** Providing the discussion questions ahead of the lesson is free and easy—it just takes a little preplanning.

- **Expectations maintained.** Students are still expected to answer the questions on their own and share their own thoughts. Providing them the questions in advance simply gives them extra processing time.

- **Equity and universality.** Discussions are richer and more informative if all students are supported in participating if they choose. Any time a student is not able to participate, then the rest of the class does not benefit from his or her ideas.

> **IF . . . THEN**
> If prequestions are used to extend the time a student has to respond to test questions, then this can also be a strategy for **Assessment.**
>
> ASSESSMENT
>

# Reading Reflection Cards

**Offer a concrete tool to support reflection while working.** A valuable skill for students to have while reading or working individually is the ability to reflect on their level of understanding or interest in the material. McGregor (2007) offered a brilliant strategy to help students express this abstract concept in a concrete way—using a paint sample strip. The cardstock strips typically have three, four, or five hues of color in a row, from lightest to darkest. They are a concrete example of a Likert scale. Establish a scale represented by each hue that students can mark or point to as they are reading or working.

## Try This

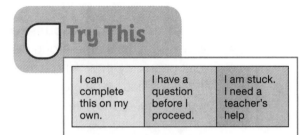

| I can complete this on my own. | I have a question before I proceed. | I am stuck. I need a teacher's help |

Reading reflection cards

## Why This Works

- **Research base.** Students' understanding while they are reading can vary. Using the cards provides them with a way to reflect on and express the extent to which they comprehend what they are reading (McGregor, 2007). The great Maxine Greene, educational philosopher, author, social activist, and teacher, believed students should be encouraged to think about their own thinking and reflection (Henderson, Hutchison, & Newman, 1998).

- **Student involvement.** Students can use the cards to reflect on their work in any content area, and they can choose three-, four-, or five-scale cards. Students can create their own descriptions for the colors on the scale and monitor their own work.

- **Reasonable use.** Paint color strips are available for no charge at most hardware and paint stores. There may even be a large amount of old cards on hand.

- **Expectations maintained.** Expressing one's level of understanding or interest is a complex skill. This strategy scaffolds mastery of that skill.

- **Equity and universality.** Students should have the choice of whether or not to use the strip to aid them, which color to use, and the number of parts in the scale.

> ► IF . . . THEN ◄
>
> If reading reflection cards are used so that students can evaluate their own level of understanding, then this can also be a strategy for **Assessment.**
>
> ASSESSMENT
>
>

# Music

**Support recall and response with music and songs.** It is nearly impossible to enter a classroom without seeing posters on the wall meant to give reminders or guide students in their work. These posters express previously learned skills the teacher intends to reinforce. In addition to visual reminders, musical reminders are also very effective. Setting information to a catchy tune or rhythm is exactly what some students need to retrieve the stored learning. Also, creating jingles, rhymes, new melodies, or new lyrics to old tunes is a way for students to express their own thoughts.

 **Try This**

Coteachers in an inclusive, third-grade classroom sing jingles to jog students' memories. Some of the jingles come from Schoolhouse Rock (http://www.schoolhouse rocklive.net/synopsis/), and the teachers have created others on their own. When a student gets stuck with a multiplication fact, for example, the teacher hums the start to the jingle, prompting the student to sing it to him- or herself until the student remembers the fact he or she needs.

## Why This Works

- **Research base.** Creating music can help express inner thoughts and feelings, and writing songs related to content allows students to express how they feel about issues they are learning about. Students can also create a simple rhythm with instruments to portray an important concept or fact (Brewer, 1995).

- **Student involvement.** Model using music as a learning and expression strategy. Engage students in helping you come up with lyrics or decide on the tune to use.

- **Reasonable use.** There are many songs on the Internet to download for free. Simply enter "classroom songs" or "educational songs" into your search field.

- **Expectations maintained.** Students are still responsible for remembering and applying knowledge and skills. Music can help them do both.

- **Equity and universality.** Use culturally relevant music and verse.

→ IF . . . THEN ◄

If music is used during instruction to facilitate the learning of new information (as suggested by Brewer, 1995), then this can also be a strategy for **Input.**

INPUT

# Drawing

**Provide students the opportunity to express themselves through drawing.** Remember the story of Tyler in the introduction to this section? Tyler (and many students like him) need to express what they know in a visual-spatial way—through drawing, rather than writing text or providing an oral explanation.

## Try This

Student drawings

## Why This Works

- **Research base.** In the book *Upside-Down Brilliance: The Visual-Spatial Learner,* Linda Kreger Silverman (2002) presents research, examples, and strategies for visual-spatial learners who process information in images rather than words.

- **Student involvement.** Once a student uses drawing to express his or her needs, if the drawing does not convey enough detail about the concept you are evaluating, talk through it with the student and have the student reflect on how details might be added—just like revising a paper.

- **Reasonable use.** It may take a little extra time to evaluate student work in drawing form if you are not used to it. Additional supplies may be needed in the classroom—colored pens and unlined paper versus pencils and lined paper.

- **Expectations maintained.** The same rubric or set of criteria can be applied to a drawing as to a written assignment—dates, quotes, vocabulary words, resource citations. Students should be given the opportunity to develop written and oral communication as well but not be deprived of the opportunity to draw.

- **Equity and universality.** Providing the opportunity to draw as a means of expression responds to students' thought processes, rather than making them respond in one particular way. To always put the burden on the student to translate his or her thinking (images) into a different format (text) is taxing for the student and exclusive.

> **→ IF . . . THEN ←**
>
> If the creation of descriptive drawings is used to assist students in learning new concepts (as research on the elaboration process from Edens & Potter, 2003, tells us), then this can also be a strategy for **Input.**
>
> INPUT
>
>

# Response Scales

**Use response scales to scaffold social skills.**
Social skills may be the most difficult thing to master in school, and they are the least often directly taught. Not all students are able to pick up social skills on their own and know how to respond in given situations. Appropriate responses are not black and white. There is a gray scale. A strategy for managing this scale is to provide a concrete version—list the options on an escalating scale. The gradients can be represented by numbers or symbols. This scale was created to help students choose the correct voice volume to use. Once they are familiar with the scale, students can be prompted with just the number.

1. *No voice:* tests, movie theater

2. *Whisper voice:* buddy reading, library

3. *Talking voice:* small-group work, [play]dates, restaurant

4. *Loud voice:* cafeteria, crowded party

5. *Yelling voice:* playground, ball game

## Try This

Must-reads

Buron, K.D. (2007). *A 5 is against the law: Social boundaries: Straight up! An honest guide for teens and young adults.* Shawnee Mission, KS: Autism Asperger Publishing.

Buron, K.D., & Curtis, M. (2012). *The incredible 5-point scale: Assisting students in understanding social situations and controlling their emotional responses* (2nd ed.). Shawnee Mission, KS: Autism Asperger Publishing.

Response scales

## Why This Works

- **Research base.** Scales such as this help create plans for self-management for students with difficulties in social thinking and emotional regulation (Buron & Curtis, 2012).

- **Student involvement.** Students should be involved in deciding which situations require the support of a scale and in the development of the scales. Reflect with students on the format that works best for them to indicate the points on the scale—numbers, letters, symbols, photos. The must-reads listed previously walk you through the development process.

- **Reasonable use.** The must-reads are available for approximately $20 each. Creating your own scales is free but takes time to develop with students.

- **Expectations maintained.** Students should not be excused from inappropriate social-emotional responses, but they should not be punished for them either. Mistakes in social skills, just like any other area, are teachable moments.

*(continued)*

- **Equity and universality.** Everyone has the right to develop meaningful, valuable relationships.

➤ IF . . . THEN ◄

If response scales are used to build social relationships and help students feel at ease in the learning environment, then this can also be a strategy for **Engagement.**

ENGAGEMENT

# Mix-Freeze-Pair

**Use Mix-Freeze-Pair to encourage conversations with different peers.** During class discussion, some students may be reluctant to contribute in front of the large group. Pairing students to communicate their ideas provides a safer audience for sharing and refining ideas before they are then shared with the class as a whole. Mix-Freeze-Pair is one strategy for this paired discussion that provides opportunities for students to interact with many different classmates over time. The steps, as described by Candler are as follows:

- When the teacher announces "Mix!" students move around the classroom.

- When the teacher calls "Freeze!" the students stop where they are.

- When the teacher calls, "Pair!" the students find the nearest partner.

- The teacher announces the topic or task for each pair to discuss or complete. (2000, p. 12)

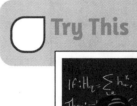

Mix-Freeze-Pair

## Why This Works

- **Research base.** Candler (2000) explained that this strategy increases opportunities for communication and discussion and provides for a great energizer after periods of sitting still.

- **Student involvement.** Students actively pair up with other students and decide together how to complete the given task.

- **Reasonable use.** Once students are given clear instructions and have had an opportunity to practice, this strategy is quick and easy to use any time.

- **Expectations maintained.** Expectations must be outlined so that students do not gravitate toward the same partner during every mix time. Also, students are expected to complete the task at hand, not only socialize during the pair time.

- **Equity and universality.** All mobility and communication supports in the classroom are used during this activity so that all students can fully participate and interact with any other student in the classroom.

→ IF . . . THEN ◄

If Mix-Freeze-Pair is used so that students have the opportunity to learn new perspectives and ideas from different sources in the classroom, then this can also be a strategy for **Input**.

INPUT

# Rally Table

**Use Rally Table for enhanced communication of ideas.** Like Mix-Freeze-Pair, Rally Table (created by Kagan, 2008) provides an opportunity for students to express their ideas and new learning via peer discussion, but it also provides a way to increase the size of the audience from one partner to three other group members. The steps are as follows:

- Teams of four are created, with two pairs in each team.

- The teacher sets an open-ended task and allows time for students to work individually to complete the task.

- When time is called, individuals work with their partners to share their ideas and build on them.

- When time is called again, two sets of partners join together as a team of four to share ideas and further build on them. They then decide whether they will work as a group of four, in pairs, or individually to finalize the task.

Rally Table

## Why This Works

- **Research base.** Based on Kagan's (2008) cooperative learning structures, this strategy is one way to increase student response and help them build communication skills, engage with more peers, and increase accountability for their learning.

- **Student involvement.** Students are scaffolded in their involvement with a partner, then a small group. They decide together how to complete the task and to evaluate their own and each other's ideas.

- **Reasonable use.** This strategy takes more preparation and practice than Mix-Freeze-Pair or other partner strategies. Take the time to instruct and model cooperative discussions in which everyone has a role and is accountable for the learning.

- **Expectations maintained.** All students in the group should be expected to contribute to the discussion and the final product.

- **Equity and universality.** All mobility, communication, reading, and writing supports used in the classroom are used during cooperative learning so that all students can participate and communicate with any other student.

→ IF . . . THEN ←

If Rally Table is used so that students have an opportunity to self-reflect, reflect with a partner, reflect with a small group, then have a final product be evaluated by the teacher, then this can also be a strategy for **Assessment.**

ASSESSMENT

# Rubrics

**Use a pie chart rubric.** Many rubrics for assignments are in list form. These types of rubrics may include all of the parts that are due for an assignment and all of the point values. However, a student who has difficulties with executive functions may also need support to figure out how much time and effort each piece will entail. A pie chart rubric offers a visual for the student to scaffold the skill of breaking down a long-term assignment and planning the time needed for each step. Chart Maker App (available for Mac or PC) easily converts lists of values into many types of visual graphs.

**Try This**

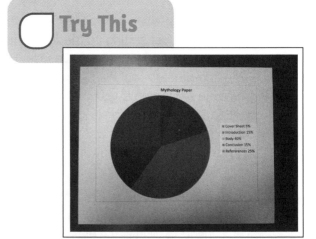

Pie chart rubric

## Why This Works

- **Research base.** Executive functioning dysfunction has a growing research base. Provision of graphic organizers and visual prompts is an effective strategy to make the learning process as concrete as possible (Dendy, 2008; Willis, 2006).

- **Student involvement.** Students can be involved in evaluating effectiveness of using the pie rubric versus a list-type rubric. Students can create their own ideas for rubrics.

- **Reasonable use.** Using a pie chart rubric is flexible and reasonable for the teacher and/or students to implement. It takes the same amount of time to create as a list rubric.

- **Expectations maintained.** Each student still writes the paper on his or her own and is evaluated on the same level of mastery for each step.

- **Equity and universality.** All students can have the choice of which rubric to use. Rubrics provide the same information for all students, whether or not they need the long-term planning and time management scaffold.

→ IF . . . THEN ←

If rubrics are used so that students can be evaluated primarily on their knowledge of the content and their writing skills, not overly on their executive functioning abilities, then this can also be a strategy for **Assessment.**

ASSESSMENT

# Templates

**Use templates whenever possible.** For some students, just setting up the format for a written response is a highly cognitive task. For example, putting the correct heading on a paper can be as much work as the task that follows. For other students, this comes naturally and requires very little extra effort. To support students who find formatting a challenge, provide templates for written work.

**Try This**

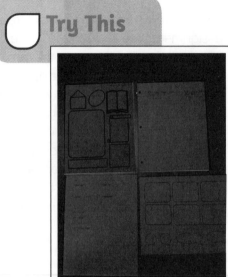

Templates

- *Preheaded papers:* If a particular heading is required, provide the students with blank paper that already has the heading at the top. All they would need to fill in is the date. Very little effort is needed, and they can get right to work on the assignment.

- *Template for components that do not change:* If students will be completing the same assignments on different topics, they can use templates for all of the sections of the assignment that are the same. For example, a college student who is studying to be a teacher and struggles with spelling, mechanics, and editing uses a lesson plan template. He created the sentence starters for each part of the lesson plan so that he would not have to rewrite these each time. Then, he just needs to complete the parts of each lesson that change—less to write and proofread.

- *Rubber stamps:* For visuals, such as graph axes, analog clock faces, or T-charts, you can purchase rubber stamps that place the template right onto the student's paper.

- *Storyboard templates:* For students who express their learning through drawing or comic form, provide sheets with boxes and speech bubble blanks. Effort can be focused on drawing and writing captions.

## Why This Works

- **Research base.** Executive functions include inhibition, shift, emotional control, initiation, working memory, planning, organization, and self-monitoring. Someone with executive function difficulties will have trouble planning and executing all of the parts of a project (Cooper-Kahn & Dietzel, 2008).

- **Student involvement.** If you notice that a student is consistently having difficulty with the format of a task, involve him or her in a discussion about making it easier to get that part out of the way using a template.

- **Reasonable use.** It only takes a little time to create each template. Then they can be copied or posted on your classroom web site.

- **Expectations maintained.** One of the most frequent responses I receive when I suggest using templates to teachers is that it would be doing the work for the student. A shift is needed in the way we think about what work is truly crucial to do. The format is not the work. The academic task that follows is the work. Providing a format template does not do the work for students, it supports them in doing the work for themselves.

- **Equity and universality.** This is an example of a strategy that levels the field so that no one has an unfair disadvantage. If formatting is a highly cognitive, draining task, then requiring it of a student doubles his or her workload. If you do not provide a strategy (a template), you are requiring those students to do twice the work of other students. Fair is not every student doing the exact same thing. Fair is students doing equitable things.

**IF . . . THEN**

If the templates cue the student to the work that is required, then this can also be a strategy for **Input.**

INPUT

# Visual Reminders

**Provide visual reminders.** Do you feel like a broken record sometimes, constantly reminding the same students about the same things—wear your glasses, bring your permission slip, you need sneakers and a water bottle for gym class. If students have a difficult time remembering the little things, they should not have to depend on you to be a constant reminder for them. Create a reminder they can have with them that supports them in being more independent. For example

**Try This**

Luggage tags and bookmark

- *Luggage tag reminders:* Print a miniature checklist of items that need to be packed, insert it into a sturdy luggage name tag, and attach it to the student's gym bag or backpack.

- *Desktop reminders:* Place a card or strip on the student's desk that has written or pictorial reminders about the school day—glasses, music lesson, permission slip due tomorrow.

- *Bookmarks:* Make bookmarks with your photo and a place to write reminders. Place them in planners, textbooks, or independent reading books. When the students open their books at home, "you" are there reminding them.

## Why This Works

- **Research base.** Kluth and Danaher (2010) described the use of luggage tags as an effective differentiation strategy.

- **Student involvement.** Students can make their own checklists and choose their own luggage tags.

- **Reasonable use.** This strategy is so easy and just about free. Luggage tags are available at the dollar store, and many companies have them as give-aways for advertising.

- **Expectations maintained.** Students are still acting independently. You are not completing the task for them; you are finding a way to support them in remembering to do it themselves.

- **Equity and universality.** All students can have reminders about something—this is universally helpful!

**→ IF . . . THEN ←**

If visual reminders are used so that students can self-monitor or self-assess whether they are ready for the day, then this can also be a strategy for **Assessment.**

ASSESSMENT

# Visual Presentation of Goals

**Have students display their IEP and transition goals visually.** Students are members of their own IEP teams. As such, they have a role in running annual meetings. When it comes to planning their transition from school to adult life, their role in the meetings can be maximized if they have a visual to present:

- *Presentation software slides:* Students can create a slide for each part of the IEP, depicting present skills and future goals.

- *Storyboard:* Students can create a storyboard or even a book showing them in each setting in the community, higher education, and living.

Students in the Postsecondary Program at St. John Fisher High School create collages of photos, text, their own drawings, and brochures to display their person-centered plans for the future.

### Try This

Visual presentation of goals

## Why This Works

- **Research base.** Being an active participant in the transition process is part of developing self-determination skills that will help students experience positive adult outcomes once they leave school (Wehmeyer & Schwartz, 1997).

- **Student involvement.** Creating visual presentations scaffolds student involvement in their own IEP meetings and transition planning. They are not just there to answer a few questions or approve what others are planning. They are there to run the meeting and present a visual display of their plans.

- **Reasonable use.** This strategy requires only teaching time to scaffold students in creating and communicating their plan.

- **Expectations maintained.** Students should be expected to increase their involvement in their IEP meetings and planning over several years so that they are ready to be active participants in transition planning by the start of the high school years.

*(continued)*

- **Equity and universality.** This strategy is the essence of the philosophy that nothing should be planned for a person without the person present, as portrayed in the saying, "Nothing about me without me."

IF . . . THEN

If visual displays of goals are used as part of a portfolio of achieved skills, then this can also be a strategy for **Assessment.**

ASSESSMENT

# Strategies for Assessment...

# PROVIDING MULTIPLE MEANS OF ASSESSMENT

UDL, as originally proposed, includes the three principles we have covered so far: engagement, input, and output. Although there is a great deal of overlap with multiple means for action and expression (in fact, it was difficult to write the Strategies for Output section without constantly talking about assessment), it is important that assessment be covered separately. Even with multiple means of action and expression, there can be a great deal of variety in the way the actions and expressions are evaluated or judged for competence. I can think of many times when working with teachers that I have heard statements such as

- "I understand that he needs to express himself in a different way, but I can't let him get used to that because he can't do it that way on the test."

- "I get that she needs extra processing time, but I don't accept late assignments."

- "Drawing is okay for homework, but not for tests."

- "We need to meet to brainstorm accommodations for her because I won't accept homework via email."

- "I know he has problems focusing for more than 15 minutes, but letting him take his test over multiple days will give him an unfair advantage over the other students and throw off the bell curve."

- "If I grade her against different criteria, I would have to do that for everyone."

This section of the book, as it addresses all of the issues just listed, may be the most important section because universally designing the other three areas is worthless if we resort to such traditional, narrowly defined assessment methods and attitudes. The strategies in this section reflect a balance of different areas of assessment: formal and informal assessments; formative and summative assessments; and alternate assessments, such as performance, portfolio, and self-assessments.

## Formal and Informal Assessments

Formal assessments are research-based, published assessments normed on a large group of participants in a given demographic. Statistical analysis generates the degree to which a formal assessment is valid (i.e., it tests what it purports to test) and reliable (i.e., it yields the same results regardless of environmental factors). Formal assessments can be given to one student at a time (e.g., the Stanford-Binet Intelligence Scales [Roid, 2003], the Woodcock-Johnson Achievement Tests [Woodcock, McGrew, & Maher, 2003], the Key Math [Connolly, 2007]). They can also be given across a large group of students at the same time (e.g., the College Board Scholastic Assessment Tests [SATs (College Board, 2013)], the New York State Regents exams [New York State Education Department, 2013], the California Standards Tests [STAR, 2013]).

Informal assessments are those that are not researched and normed on groups of participants. They are typically created by the teacher and used only with his or her students to inform daily practice. Weekly spelling tests, worksheets, and projects with rubrics are examples of informal assessments.

## Formative and Summative Assessments

Formative assessments are those that teachers use during lessons (usually teacher-created, informal assessments) to see how students are performing along the way—how student progress is forming. If the results of a formative assessment indicate that the students do not yet have a concept mastered or that they are developing misconceptions, the teacher uses the assessment results to modify instruction. Formative assessments can be given in any area—academic, social, physical, and behavioral. Formative assessments can be written (e.g., homework paper, quiz, worksheets) or oral (e.g., asking discussion questions, observing small-group collaboration).

Summative assessments are generally used at the end of a unit of study or grade level to see what the students know and can do after instruction has taken place—how student progress has summed up. Summative assessments are typically written, completed individually in a timed and controlled setting (i.e., test). Summative assessments can be teacher-created and individualized to a certain classroom, but they are sometimes formal and standardized to be used across schools, districts, states, or even the nation to determine how students compare with others on the same content. There is a great deal of criticism surrounding issues of using standardized summative assessment results to judge teacher effectiveness or school quality (Rapp & Arndt, 2012).

## Alternative Assessments

Alternative assessments provide information about student performance and applied knowledge and skills in ways other than typical written tests. They tend to be more authentic, contextualized, meaningful, and based on individual learning goals. They are also more time-consuming to create, use, and evaluate than traditional written tests.

*Performance Assessment*   Performance assessments evaluate students as they actually perform a given task while observed by the evaluator. Driving tests to obtain your license and student teaching are both examples of performance assessments.

*Portfolio Assessment*   A portfolio assessment is a collection of evidence that demonstrates the range of knowledge and skills that a student has mastered. Representative products are included in the portfolio, but the actual performance is not observed firsthand by the teacher. So, rather than observing actual driving, the teacher might evaluate the written report from the driving test that was included in the portfolio. Rather than observing live teaching, the teacher may evaluate a videotaped lesson or a written lesson plan that was included in the portfolio.

*Self-Assessment*   Self-assessments are completed by the student. Monitoring and evaluating one's own progress is difficult and takes a great deal of practice to do effectively. Reflective journals, self-questionnaires, checklists, and rating scales are a few types of self-assessments. The teacher may be part of the assessment as the student learns how to become more effective at self-evaluation, but the student is always involved, too.

## CONSIDERATIONS

When creating multiple means of assessment for students, there are many considerations to keep in mind.

## Teaching to the Test

Teachers can often be heard voicing their concerns that they do not have time to do the effective activities they used to do because they have to spend so much time preparing students for state and national standardized tests. The assumption here is that only practicing the test content in the test format will prepare students for the test. The content on these tests can be taught in a myriad of ways, one of which can be the format of the test. Students are much more likely to understand and be able to apply the concepts if they learn them and express them in many different ways. If one of these ways is the test format and vocabulary, then students will be familiar with and ready to meet the expectations of the test. In essence, it is not an either/or situation—either you prepare them for the test *or* you provide UDL. Instead, UDL should *include* preparing them for the test.

Willis (2006) explained it like this: When teachers reinforce learning in different ways and help students find meaning and connections with the new information, the brain processes and stores the information in relational patterns. Once these patterns are formed, the information can be accessed by multiple cues, brought to the frontal lobe, and applied to various situations—including responses on standardized tests.

## View of Mastery and Success

We put all students at a disadvantage by thinking that there is one measure of success in school (i.e., grades) or one set of skills that are necessary for success in school (e.g., homework in on time, high test scores, neat work, no behavior problems, strong reading and writing skills). We also put all students at a disadvantage when we compare students with each other to decide if they are succeeding (i.e., the bell curve). We need to shift our thinking about valuable skills for success in and out of school. Are the most valuable skills reading, writing, and speaking, or are they problem-solving, critical thinking, leadership and collaboration, and self-determination? We also need to shift our thinking about how we determine when a student has mastered a concept or skill. Is it when he can do it better than most of his classmates, or is it when he can do it independently and apply it effectively in appropriate situations, regardless of what his classmates are doing?

## The Right to Fail or Make Mistakes

The purpose of UDL is not to make sure that everyone passes every time or always gets an *A*. The purpose is to create equitable opportunity for everyone to approach, have access to, and learn the necessary content. Think back to the analogy in Section I that school is like a hike. Our role is to open the gate to the hiking path, remove the big rocks from the students' backpacks (in different, research-based, culturally responsive ways), and stand on the sidelines encouraging them along the way. After that, the student has the right to hike or not.

Here is one example. A ninth-grade student who struggles with executive functioning difficulties was spending a great deal of effort and time managing all of the new demands of high school—more readings from different sources (textbooks, articles, web sites), more long-term assignments on top of daily short-term assignments, and pop quizzes. He often sat down at home in the evening to do homework only to find that he had the wrong materials, misinformation written in his planner, and no idea what to work on for each subject so that it all got done. Because it was determined that these difficulties were all manifestations of a disability, he was entitled to support. Teachers, parents, and the student collaboratively figured out which were the big rocks he was carrying and how to remove them so that he was exerting equitable effort in completing the work as his peers, rather than using up all of his energy on time and material management. Supports were put in place—extra books at home, all materials and assignments posted on the classroom web site, extra time, assignments sent by email. This helped tremendously. The times he used his supports, he was successful obtaining access to the information and expressing his learning. The times he did not use his supports, he was not successful. This is okay because the opportunity is equitable. He has every right to experience failure or lack of success and learn from the consequences, just like anyone else. He has every right *not* to check the web site for the needed materials. However, if they were never posted, he would not have had the right *to* check the web site. There would have been no choice, and that would have been exclusionary.

## Need for Effective Feedback

Tomlinson and McTighe (2006) noted that effective feedback must be timely, specific, and understandable, and it must provide an opportunity for adjustment. To some students, it is a mystery as to how they are progressing. If this is the case, they are missing valuable opportunities for self-reflection, modification, and growth. In order to learn, we need to receive quick feedback so that the thought processes we used for the task are fresh in our minds and ripe for rethinking. We also need to have clear details about what needs to be improved and also what is going well. A symbolic grade means nothing if we cannot tie it to details about the quality of work or alignment to expectations. Feedback that leads to meaningful learning is used to provide an opportunity to reflect and redo. If we cannot change anything and then receive more feedback, our efforts are meaningless and disconnected from any authentic application.

## How It All Comes Together

All of the foundational theories contribute significantly to the understanding of effective, universally designed assessment. Tomlinson and McTighe (2006) urged us to remember that understanding should be assessed before teaching; appropriate choices of assessment, all with a common set of criteria, should be offered; self-assessment and reflection should be encouraged; and feedback should be provided early and often. In addition, they offered three principles of assessment. First, assessments are most reliable when multiple measures are considered. Student progress cannot effectively be evaluated though a single piece of evidence. To use their analogy, assessment is a photo album, not a snapshot. Second, the type of assessment used should match the goal of the learning. To know if students can drive a car, you need to see them drive a car. It would be silly to have them write a paper about driving. This is an extreme example, but there are many assessments used in schools today that no better match the measure with the goal. Student understanding is evaluated when knowledge and skills are applied in authentic contexts. Third, form follows function. Once we know why we are assessing and how we will use the assessment results, we can then figure how to assess. Applied to grading and reporting grades, if we decide first on the form (e.g., letter grades on reports cards), we risk putting more importance on the symbols rather than on the growth they represent. Grading and reporting should be the best way to communicate a complex process of planning, instruction, assessment, student progress, more planning and instruction, further assessment, and progress. It should tell the whole story, not just be "the end."

On the subject of grades and test scores, Gay (2010) asserted that they are symptoms, not causes of or solutions for achievement. Grades and scores do not tell us *why* students are performing the way they are. In order to do this, we need to disaggregate assessment data, seek patterns across students who perform at certain levels, and meet their individual needs. To be responsive to diversity, assessment needs to be individualized, not standardized.

Research that tells us that the brain likes certain things when it comes to assessment and feedback. First, predictability is very important. Predictable sequences of behavior and response nourish the brain's penchant for patterns, facilitating it to work efficiently. Rubrics are an excellent tool to use to ensure predictability. Students know what is expected and how the teacher plans to respond, and they have a resource for monitoring their response along the way. Second, specific feedback is important. Explaining *why* the work is good or the artwork is pretty is motivating. Third, students should not be compared with each other. The bell curve, a display of where students rank in relation to the whole group, facilitates negative thinking about performance, decreasing memory storage and learning. If students are encouraged to look at only their own performance and growth over time, the positive reinforcement releases dopamine in the brain for optimal encoding of new data. We basically learn better when we feel good about ourselves, and we feel bad about ourselves if we are stacked up against one another (Willis, 2006).

Ranking students as is done with the bell curve serves to segregate students, quite the opposite of working toward inclusion and full citizenship (Kliewer, 1998). When we rank students, we are saying there is one quality, characteristic, or achievement that is valued, and some people have it more than others. Both the value and the way this quality, characteristic, or achievement is assessed are typically decided on by people who have it. In this way, a narrow view of success is perpetuated.

The strategies in this section are ways to make assessment more meaningful, authentic, engaging, informative, and positive for students, teachers, and families. The format of this section is a little different from the previous three. Strategies are presented for testing, homework, performance assessment, portfolio assessment, and self-assessment.

# Adapted Tests

**Adapt tests for accessibility and accurate evaluation.** If you do use tests to assess students' knowledge, skills, and understanding, it is important to adapt the test for their needs. If a student faces barriers gaining access to the test questions and directions or responding, then you will not have an accurate evaluation of the student's understanding of the content. Rather, you will be evaluating how the student maneuvers the test. The test should not stand in the way of student expression; it should facilitate it. Kluth and Danaher (2010) suggested the following adaptations as appropriate for a student's reading level, expressive ability, individualized goals, and physical needs:

- Dictate the directions and test items.

- Record the student's oral responses.

- Reduce the number of test items or multiple-choice options.

- Provide the answers and have the student match them to test questions.

- Allow the student to illustrate responses.

- Allow open books or notes.

- Provide sample answers.

- Add visuals to the directions and test items.

- Highlight key directions or words.

- Enlarge the print.

- Include larger spaces between test items or sections of the test.

Another way to adapt tests is to administer them on the computer. By using computer hardware adaptations (see p. 129), flexible fonts, print size, spacing, and speech-to-text or text-to-speech software, the test is accessible to any user and provides multiple means of expression (Salend, 2009).

Cassie Pruitt, a high school English teacher, suggests allowing students to take a test and then indicate which answers they would like graded. For example, have them choose their best three short answers out of five, then only assess students on those three.

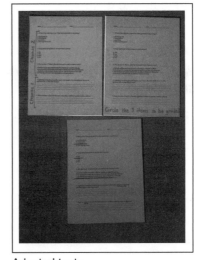

Adapted tests

*(continued)*

# Why This Works

- **Research base.** "Good assessment often calls for the use of different tools and products" (Wormeli, 2006, p. 40). Wormeli (2006) offers extensive support in creating good test questions.

- **Student involvement.** Students should be involved in determining the most appropriate form and criteria and in reflecting on adaptations they may need to have access to the test.

- **Reasonable use.** Adapting premade tests or creating your own differentiated tests takes extensive time and planning, but there is no cost.

- **Expectations maintained.** Adapting tests shifts the expectations of students to where they should be—demonstrating knowledge, skills, and understanding—not on tackling the test format.

- **Equity and universality.** Anything that is put in place for the student to engage with, learn, and express learning should be put in place in a testing situation.

→ IF . . . THEN ←

If adapted tests are used to help students express what they have mastered, then this can also be a strategy for **Output.**

OUTPUT

# Retesting

**Allow students to retake tests.** The reason we test students is to find out what they know. We want to have information about what they are taking with them after instruction. For students who struggle with test taking (e.g., anxiety, extra processing time), the results on one test will not provide us with a true assessment of everything they have learned about. It will tell us how much they were able to impart in one sitting. One of Paula Kluth's tips of the day (http://www.paulakluth .com) is to allow students to take a test more than once. After they have had a chance to see what the test is like and the types of questions they will be asked, give them a day to digest it and go through it again the next day. Once the anxiety (or simply curiosity) about the test format, length, and difficulty, for example, is relieved, they will be better able to demonstrate all they know. To alleviate stress and discouragement about testing, Willis (2006) used test correction sheets as a passport to retest. The correction sheets challenge students to reflect on their performance and express what should have been done differently. Upon retesting, students demonstrate a greater level of mastery coupled with higher self-esteem.

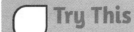 **Try This**

I recommend adding one question at the end of any test: "Is there anything else you would like to say about what you learned?" This question should not be graded, but the response could be used to supplement answers to other questions. Responses to this open-ended question have often provided me with much more insight as to what students are taking away with them than any other test question I have developed.

## Why This Works

- **Research base.** Retesting motivates students to keep working because they see a direct correlation between practice and success (Willis, 2006).

- **Student involvement.** Retesting provides an opportunity for self- and metacognition. Students are able to contribute valuable information to their overall evaluation.

- **Reasonable use.** In most situations, allowing students to retest entails one more day for students to reflect. Much more time is saved in the long run from remediating students who were moved along to the next unit before mastery of the previous one.

- **Expectations maintained.** Some teachers consider this cheating because the student sees the test, can study more, can change answers, and may do better. If the student is reflecting, learning more material, and better expressing that learning, who is being cheated?

- **Equity and universality.** This strategy separates evaluation of student knowledge, skills, and understanding from testing barriers.

→ IF . . . THEN ←

If retesting is used as a means of representing and reinforcing new learning, then this can also be a strategy for **Input.**

INPUT

# Computer Practice Tests

**Provide computer practice tests.** In the introduction to this section, I discussed the importance of reinforcing conceptual learning in many different ways, including the test format, to familiarize students with the test without solely teaching to the test. Practice tests are an example of this. They can be used to show students what the test questions, format, and length will be like after the material was learned through multiple means of input. There are web sites that will generate sample tests on particular topics or units of study and will provide immediate feedback to students.

## Try This

Computer practice tests

Here are two examples:

* Castle Learning Online: https://www.castlelearning.com/review/castlesoftware/home.aspx

* The Princeton Review: http://www.princetonreview.com/free-online-practice-tests.aspx

## Why This Works

* **Research base.** Computer practice tests can reduce test anxiety because the more familiar you are with sitting for a length of time and pacing yourself as you work through the test questions, the more comfortable you will become with the actual test (Educational Testing Service, 2005).

* **Student involvement.** Computer practice tests are completed independently by students wherever they can access the Internet and log on to the practice site. On some sites, they can choose the types of questions (e.g., multiple choice, essay) and the length of the practice test.

* **Reasonable use.** Some sites require a subscription fee, usually paid by the school, which can run anywhere from $1 to $10 per student. Other sites are free. There is no extra work for the teacher because the site evaluates the practice test and provides feedback.

* **Expectations maintained.** Students are evaluated on what they learned without being surprised by or unfamiliar with the test format.

* **Equity and universality.** All computer adaptations can be used for the practice tests.

> → IF . . . THEN ←
>
> If computer practice tests are used as another means of reinforcing the content to be learned, then this can also be a strategy for **Input.**
>
> INPUT
> ⊕

# Activities with Products

**Assess students through activities with products.** Who says tests must be pen-and-paper format, oral exams, or even on the computer? Why not assess students on the outcome of a class activity? Have students play a board game and observe their performance on certain skills (e.g., counting spaces, making change, making strategic decisions). Modify existing games to practice needed skills (e.g., replace cards in Trivial Pursuit, solve math problems on checkers that are jumped, add a spelling or vocabulary word to each Sorry card). Kagan Brain-Based Learning Tools (http://www.kaganonline.com/catalog/brain_based_learning.php) makes a large dice cube with performance tasks written on each side. Fly swatters make good buzzers. When students slap the same surface, it is obvious whose landed first, and it adds a bodily kinesthetic element—although students should have the choice to participate in a game like this. Educational Learning Games (http://www.educationallearninggames.com) is another helpful web site.

**Try This**

Activities with products

## Why This Works

- **Research base.** Silverman (2002) shared that games can be used to develop and assess auditory processing skills.

- **Student involvement.** Students can decide which skill they will work on while playing a game or interacting with an educational product (e.g., "I am going to add the numbers on the dice together") or create their own modified game cards or rules.

- **Reasonable use.** Games can be purchased for $5–$30 dollars. By spending $50 a year, you can build an extensive library over time. Scour garage sales and thrift stores as well.

- **Expectations maintained.** There must be a mechanism in place to evaluate individual student versus group performance. For example, have each student collect the cards he or she is able to answer correctly.

- **Equity and universality.** This strategy recognizes that not everyone is able to express his or her learning the same way, and pen-and-paper tests, oral questioning, or computer formats may not get at all of the skills a student has mastered.

→ IF . . . THEN ◀

If these activities are used as social, cooperative learning activities that do not feel like an assessment, then this can also be a strategy for **Engagement.**

ENGAGEMENT

# Entry and Exit Responses

**Give students surveys in the door and tickets out the door.** There is a very quick and effective way to administer pre- and postassessments for each class or lesson. At the beginning or end of a lesson, or as students enter or exit the classroom, conduct a 1-minute survey. Put one to three questions on a half-sheet of paper that students can answer briefly. For example

- I think iambic pentameter is...

- One word I use to describe poetry is...

- Circle one: I would rather write poems, play music, or observe bugs.

You can ask the same questions at the beginning and end to assess the difference in learning or perspectives, or you can ask new questions at the end. If there are misconceptions on exit tickets, you can provide feedback on the question sheets and hand them back the next day, or you can share exemplar responses so that students have the correct information.

## Try This

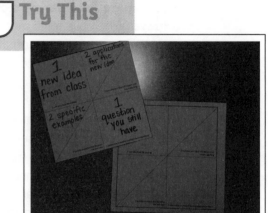

Reflection sheet

## Why This Works

- **Research base.** The process of summarizing the main points of a lesson boosts memory because it makes a learning connection that grows new dendrites (Willis, 2006).

- **Student involvement.** Students can be in charge of making sure everyone is given a survey at the beginning of a lesson and reminding you to leave a minute at the end of the lesson so that they can complete the exit survey—I often rely on my students for this reminder! Students can also submit ideas for survey questions.

- **Reasonable use.** The survey sheets are simple to make and copy in advance.

- **Expectations maintained.** If there are misconceptions, be sure to provide feedback and/or expect students to resubmit a corrected response.

- **Equity and universality.** Surveys can be put up on the interactive whiteboard or posted on the class web site so that students can complete them using their adaptations, if needed.

→ IF ... THEN ←

If entry and exit responses are used so that students can express the main idea of the lesson quickly in an interesting way that requires no preparation, then this can also be a strategy for **Output.**

OUTPUT

# ▯ CHOICE!

**Always offer a choice through homework menus.** I really cannot emphasize this enough, and I am sure you have noticed how often I have mentioned student choice throughout the book. Choice is essential for inclusive UDL environments in all areas—engagement, input, output, and assessment. I chose to put it as a strategy here because it seems that teachers have the hardest time making the shift to universally designing assessment (more so than engagement, input, and output), and homework seems like a good place to start making that shift. Tomlinson and McTighe (2006) emphasized the importance of establishing a common set of criteria across all options, and they recognized the seemingly disparate concept of offering different options that all have the same criteria. There are, however, so many ways to do that. Instead of thinking about homework assignments, think in terms of homework menus. Menus are just as they sound—an array of options to choose from. Consider the following examples:

 **Try This**

Must-read

Laurie Westphal's series of *Differentiated Instruction with Menus* books from Prufrock Press (http://www.prufrock.com/cw_contributorinfo.aspx?ContribID=257&Name=Laurie+E.+).

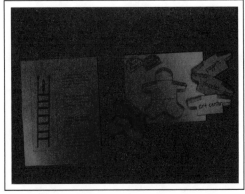
Homework menus

- A tic-tac-toe board in which students choose three homework options in a row to complete by the end of the week. This gives them choice of assignment and when they do it.

- A restaurant menu in which students must choose an appetizer, main course, dessert, and beverage.

- A checklist of options, each with varying point values, in which students must complete at least 100 points worth in any combination they choose.

## Why This Works

- **Research base.** Many theorists advocate for the absolute need for student choice (Gargiulo & Metcalf, 2010; Gay, 2010; Kliewer, 1998; Kohn, 2006; McGregor, 2007; Rapp & Arndt, 2012; Rose & Meyer, 2002; Tomlinson & McTighe, 2006; Willis, 2006; Wormeli, 2006, 2007).

- **Student involvement.** Students can submit ideas for assignments to be included on menus. After receiving specific choices to include on menus, students can create their own.

*(continued)*

- **Reasonable use.** It will take more planning time to create more ideas for homework assignments, but once this is done, the choices are ready to use over and over. Also, it may take a little more time to evaluate homework, as students will be handing in different products.

- **Expectations maintained.** No matter what students choose, they will have to meet the goal and common set of criteria established across all choices. Their choices will give you insight into their interests and strengths.

- **Equity and universality.** Wormeli (2006) cautioned to avoid "fluff" assignments. Each and every choice must be of substance and require higher level thinking skills. The choices should not be watered down, only different in format and style.

→ IF . . . THEN ←

If choice is used so that students are empowered and invested in their own learning and evaluation, then this can also be a strategy for **Engagement.**

ENGAGEMENT

# Family Projects

**Offer homework options that families do together.** Once all of my children were in school, our family was apart from each other on weekdays for the whole school year. My kids would go off to their different classes. My husband and I would go off to our different workplaces. Once everyone returned home at the end of the day, we would have dinner together (as often as possible when athletic, class, and event schedules allowed), then go off in separate ways again to do homework. This was very discouraging to me. It was a wonderful treat on the evenings when one of the kids was assigned "family homework" intended for everyone to do together. Here are several fun ideas that reinforce learning:

- Play Scrabble or Monopoly.

- Make a recipe.

- Write a family newsletter—each member contributes an item to glue on a layout.

- Make a family snapshot collage or timeline.

- Debate a controversial issue (once for us it was whether homework was beneficial!).

- Have drop-everything-and-read time.

- Solve a family problem (e.g., What color should we paint the living room? How can we have a fun vacation on a very tight budget?).

- Explore a new topic.

## Try This

**Must-read**

Kohn, A. (2006). *The homework myth: Why our kids get too much of a bad thing.* Philadelphia, PA: De Capo Press.

Family projects

## Why This Works

- **Research base.** Kohn (2006) asserted that some of the most useful ways students can spend their time at home after school hours are reading and doing activities with their families.

- **Student involvement.** The student is the cruise director for the family for some time during the evening.

- **Reasonable use.** Coming up with valuable family activities requires no more work or resources than any other assignment.

*(continued)*

- **Expectations maintained.** As with other homework choices, avoid fluff assignments. Having the whole family work on a math worksheet together, for example, is not very creative. Take the time to think of creative, cooperative activities.

- **Equity and universality.** Everyone is included. If you are part of the family, you are part of the activity. There is no one right way to do it.

> **IF . . . THEN**
>
> If family projects are used as culturally responsive, community-building activities, then this can also be a strategy for **Engagement.**
>
> ENGAGEMENT
>
>

# Peer Groups

**Allow students to complete homework in peer groups.** Like family projects, assignments completed with peer groups are a valuable alternative to traditional homework assignments. Project-based assignments such as these work best for peer groups:

Peer groups

- Research on a given topic, country, career, or concept

- An experiment to be displayed in a science fair

- Exploring multiple applications for a math concept

- Literary analysis of a book (book club)

I use Book Talks in most of my classes as a peer group assignment. I offer several choices of readings. Groups are formed by the students' choice of book to read. I give each group a list of the class days when they will have Book Talk Time and the due date for the final presentation. I also give them a packet explaining five different roles—Facilitator, who makes sure everyone gets to share; Dictionary, who defines any new or difficult words from the reading; Illustrator, who presents a visual summary of the reading; Summarizer, who shares the main points of each chapter; and Quotation Expert, who presents significant phrases for discussion. From there, the group makes its own reading assignments and role assignments and plans a final presentation of the book for the whole class.

## Why This Works

- **Research base.** Peer-mediated instruction is structured to provide scaffolds for students to construct new meaning and integrate new concepts (Kroeger et al., 2009).

- **Student involvement.** Students should decide who they are going to work with, the role of each person in the group, and how they should be evaluated.

- **Reasonable use.** Using peer groups takes more time to set up because students need support in learning how to set goals, roles, and evaluation criteria.

- **Expectations maintained.** The purpose of homework should be to reinforce learning that occurred during the school day. This reinforces the content knowledge as well as cooperative learning skills and community building.

*(continued)*

- **Equity and universality.** All students should be grouped with peers who fully include them as members in the peer group. It may mean starting with pairs for some students to meet their needs and enlisting families to help support the partnership.

 IF . . . THEN

If peer groups are used to facilitate construction of new knowledge among students, then this can also be a strategy for **Input.**

INPUT

# Family Message Journals

**Assign family message journals to assess writing for an audience.** Anytime students are writing for an authentic audience, they are engaging in performance assessment. With family message journals, the audience is the student's own family members. Family message journals are notebooks that travel between home and school daily. The students write (with any needed supports) a message to their families about the day's happenings, an upcoming school event, or other information that is important for the family to know. No other announcements or notices are sent home, thus increasing the importance and authenticity of the student's message. Family members respond in the journal and return it to school.

 **Try This**

Family message journal

## Why This Works

- **Research base.** Writing is an essential skill to acquire and assess. Family members can continue the instruction of writing at home by responding in the journal, and students learn to communicate more effectively by writing to an authentic audience (Valerie & Foss-Swanson, 2012).

- **Student involvement.** Students write the message themselves to their family members. They can decide to illustrate the message, read it to the family members, or have them read it on their own.

- **Reasonable use.** You may have to provide the notebooks to students.

- **Expectations maintained.** Students are expected to develop many skills over time—writing clear, detailed messages; delivering the journal; encouraging a response; returning the journal daily; and learning the parts of a formal letter.

- **Equity and universality.** Some families may need accommodations if they are not able to write back in a conventional way or speak a language other than the one used in the journal.

> → IF . . . THEN ←
>
> If family message journals are used to provide a culturally responsive purpose for writing, then this can also be a strategy for **Output.**
>
> OUTPUT
>
>

# Solving Real-World Problems

**Assess skills used to solve real problems in the school or the community.** An effective way to make an assessment authentic and meaningful is to assess skills that are used to make a difference in the school or community. During class meetings or anytime a student mentions frustration with a situation, turn it into an opportunity to solve the problem. Here are some examples that provide the opportunity to assess students on writing, math, and communication skills:

- Not all students have the same choice of recess activities because the school does not have adapted playground equipment. Suggest a small group of students work on a budget proposal to buy an adapted swing and climber.

- The bike racks at the high school are located next to the dumpsters in the back of the school, so there are often bees flying near the students who use them. Suggest students list the safety issues involved and plan a better place for the racks.

- Membership in some of the school clubs is restricted to certain grade levels. Suggest students write a letter to the club advisors requesting a change in policy.

- A local family has lost their belongings in a house fire. Suggest students plan a fundraiser to replace clothing and toys.

## Try This

When Benny Smith, a sixth-grader and advocate for the environment, realized that the district disposes of hundreds of polystyrene lunch trays each day, he set a goal to replace them with biodegradable trays instead. He researched the benefits to student health and the environment, calculated the cost difference, and wrote a proposal to the school board. The response was a complete switch to the eco-friendly trays!

## Why This Works

- **Research base.** One way to engage students in math activities is to provide a real-world context (Rapp, 2009).

- **Student involvement.** Students are involved in the assessment throughout the process, from identifying the problem to the steps taken to solve it.

- **Reasonable use.** Once the students identify the problem, it takes a little extra time to establish the set of criteria, guide the students through the project, and evaluate their skills.

- **Expectations maintained.** Provide students with a checklist of steps to follow or a list of information they will need to solve the problem (e.g., the address for the school board) and let them know what you will be assessing throughout the process (e.g., clarity of writing in the letter, correct mathematical calculations in the budget proposal).

- **Equity and universality.** This is an assessment that results in a more inclusive school or community.

> **→ IF . . . THEN ←**
>
> If solving real-world problems is used as a culturally responsive and meaningful connection for the students, then this can also be a strategy for **Engagement.**
>
> ENGAGEMENT

# Ability Profiles

**Create a profile of students' abilities.** An ability profile is a representation of skills that a student has achieved. The representation may be a written description, a photo, a video, or a work sample. The idea is to focus on what the student *can* do and show how far the student has come, not how far the student has to go. Before and after comparisons can illustrate the growth over time.

Kluth and Danaher (2010) offered two great examples:

Ability profiles

- *See-Me-Strong Book:* This profile displays photos of the students performing skills that they have achieved. Based on individualized goals, the skills achieved might be physical (e.g., rolling over, walking, doing jumping jacks), cognitive (e.g., reading independently), behavioral (e.g., sitting quietly during transition times, raising hand before shouting out), or social (e.g., playing a game on the playground). The finished profile is like a picture book all about the student.

- *Strengths & Strategies Profile:* This is a report of all of the student's strengths and all of the strategies that help support the student to grow further. All of the information is positive and proactive and focuses on what works.

## Why This Works

- **Research base.** The ways in which we communicate with families can either strengthen or damage the relationship (Kluth & Danaher, 2010). With ability profiles, the focus of communication with families is on a student's strengths and accomplishments. Areas of need or skills not yet accomplished are then discussed in a context of positive student support.

- **Student involvement.** Students should be involved in selecting items to be included in the ability profiles and what descriptions about the achievement should be.

- **Reasonable use.** Ability profiles take more time to prepare than typical report cards or progress reports, and they require equipment needed to take and print photos.

- **Expectations maintained.** Students are working toward the same goals and objectives, but the assessment focuses on gains.

- **Equity and universality.** All students have strengths. This assessment celebrates all students for what they are able to do.

→ IF . . . THEN ←

If ability profiles are used to remind students of details and events and reinforce concepts involved, then this can also be a strategy for **Input.**

INPUT

# Responsive Report Cards

**Use responsive report cards.** Once you have provided multiple means of engagement, input, output, and assessment, do not resort to static, uniform formats for reporting progress to families. A single grade, accompanied by one or two comments that are selected from a menu of prewritten comments, is not informative at all. It does not indicate how hard a student has worked, what coping strategies or study skills he or she learned along the way, or interests the student developed during the units of study. Report cards should indicate how far the student has progressed, how the curriculum was designed to meet his or her needs, the skills achieved, and the skills yet to be achieved. The report card should be as differentiated as the instruction, indicating not only if the student understands the concept but also to what degree he or she is able to effectively apply it in various settings.

## Try This

Responsive report cards

## Why This Works

- **Research base.** The purpose of reporting progress to families is not just to mark the current level of performance but also to evaluate the effectiveness of services that are in place (IDEA 2004).

- **Student involvement.** Students can be involved in writing the comments on the report card. You might say, "I am going to indicate that you are reading at Level H right now. What story would you like to tell about your reading so far this year?" Then, you can add any necessary information to the student's words.

- **Reasonable use.** This form of reporting will take significantly more time than a simple report card that requires a letter grade or checkmark. If progress is described throughout the assessment period, the time can be distributed reasonably.

- **Expectations maintained.** Students should be expected to be involved in their own assessment and reporting to parents. It builds advocacy skills.

- **Equity and universality.** Nothing about me without me.

> **→ IF . . . THEN ←**
>
> If responsive report cards are used as prompts to help students express their needs and accomplishments, then this can also be a strategy for **Output.**
>
> OUTPUT
>
>

#  "I Can..." Sheets

**Have students complete "I can..." sheets.**
To help students develop self-awareness of their knowledge and skills and to prompt them toward additional help in areas of need, guide them in the use of a self-assessment for each concept you are teaching in class. Written descriptions with a visual Likert scale scaffold their efforts. This could also be used for an entrance or exit ticket.

| "I can..." | 😀 | 😐 | 🙁 |
|---|---|---|---|
| Find my home state on a map of the United States. | | | |
| Name the capital of my home state. | | | |
| Name the governor of my home state. | | | |
| Explain the responsibilities of the governor. | | | |
| Explain one issue that the governor should consider. | | | |

"I can..." sheet.

## Why This Works

- **Research base.** "Goals, effort, achievement, self-judgment, and self-reaction all can combine to impact self-confidence in a positive way. Self-evaluation is really the combination of the self-judgment and self-reaction components of the model, and if we can teach students to do this better we can contribute to an upward cycle of better learning" (Rolheiser & Ross, n.d., p. 1).

- **Student involvement.** Students evaluate themselves and develop ownership of the content that is required of them.

- **Reasonable use.** Using "I can..." sheets is a simple, quick assessment that can be completed in or outside of class. It is easy to model for students, then scaffold them to use it independently.

- **Expectations maintained.** The students are not only expected to master the content, they are made aware of their progress along the way.

- **Equity and universality.** All students can make use of these sheets even if they need support.

> **IF ... THEN**
>
> "I can..." sheets are used to provide students with a list of concepts they are expected to know, and if the content for a particular unit is laid out for them as a resource, then this can also be a strategy for **Input.**
>
> **INPUT**

# Learning Logs

**Encourage students to keep learning logs.** A learning log is simply an individual journal or notebook in which students record ideas or reflections on what they are learning. Provide a choice of materials for the logs—lined paper, drawing paper, graph paper—and a choice of completing it on paper or on the computer. Provide regular opportunities for students to update their journals. In the beginning of the year, students can be scaffolded with prompts to get them started. The logs can be interactive as well, with the teacher commenting on each of the students' entries with encouragement and suggestions.

**Try This**

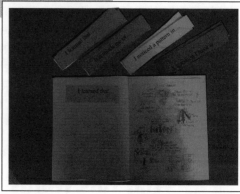

Learning logs

Some of the prompts suggested by Wormeli (2006) include

- I learned that…

- An insight I have gained is…

- I liked/did not like…

- I noticed a pattern in…

- I cannot understand…

- It reminds me of…

- I would like to learn more about…

## Why This Works

- **Research base.** Wormeli (2006) emphasized the value of learning logs and interactive notebooks as self-assessment tools. Self-evaluation has the potential to have an impact on student performance through enhanced self-efficacy and intrinsic motivation (Rolheiser & Ross, n.d.).

- **Student involvement.** Students should choose the format and the prompt to use. The students can also decide if the entry is private or can be read and commented on by the teacher.

- **Reasonable use.** Learning logs are very easy to implement and take no more time to evaluate than other homework assignments.

- **Expectations maintained.** Students are learning knowledge and skills, along with self-evaluation and reflection skills.

- **Equity and universality.** Be sure to provide a format that every student can use to express him- or herself.

> **→ IF . . . THEN ←**
>
> If learning logs are used as an alternative way for students to express their thoughts and ideas about their own learning experiences, then this can also be a strategy for **Output.**
>
> OUTPUT
>
>

# IRS Questions

**List IRS questions for students to answer.** IRS questions were coined by Kluth and Danaher (2010) to describe a list of reminder questions posed to students so that they can double check themselves—as the IRS does to remind you to double check everything before submitting your tax return. You can have IRS questions on the spot where students submit work (e.g., "Did you put your name on your paper?" "Did you show your work?"). You also can put them in a student's locker (e.g., "Did you put your lunchbox back in your bag?" "Do you have your materials to study for the test?").

At one middle school I visited, a teacher had stretched masking tape across the doorway to her classroom, right in the middle where students could not possibly enter without noticing it. From the masking tape was a bright sheet of paper asking, "Do you have your book? Do you have a pencil?"

Try This

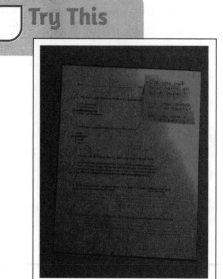

IRS questions

## Why This Works

- **Research base.** Using IRS questions can alleviate frustration because the students have the opportunity to catch their mistakes before they are left empty handed (Kluth & Danaher, 2010).

- **Student involvement.** Students can create their own IRS questions on a checklist or sticky note as a self-reminder. Students can even write IRS questions for the teacher (e.g., "Did you select a new read-aloud book?").

- **Reasonable use.** One minute to write out the questions saves many minutes of students retracing steps, returning to lockers, and so forth.

- **Expectations maintained.** Using IRS questions is a great support that some students need so that they can be expected to be as independent as their peers.

- **Equity and universality.** Everyone needs a reminder. This strategy provides one to every student in the class equitably. If you can already answer "yes" to all of the questions, you are all set. If you answer "no," you have an opportunity to get caught up.

→ IF ... THEN ←

If IRS questions are used so that students can act independently to take care of their own needs and responsibilities, then this can also be a strategy for **Output.**

OUTPUT

# Three Cups

**Provide three colored cups for students to indicate their level of understanding.** During a lesson, teachers often assess understanding by asking questions or scanning the crowd for confused faces. Another way to determine who is comfortable with the content, who is confused, or who is frustrated is to implement the three-cups system. Each student has three cups stacked on his or her desk—one green, one yellow, and one red. If the green one is on top, it indicates the student understands the information and does not have a question. If the yellow one is on top, the student may be a little confused, needs another example, or needs to slow down. If the red one is on top, the student is frustrated or really needs a break. The cups can be used continually during the lesson

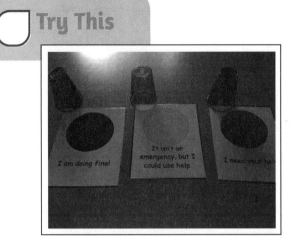

Try This

Three cups

or at checkpoints when the teacher stops and asks how everyone is doing. Likewise, when students are working independently while the teacher circulates, a green cup indicates no help is needed, a yellow cup indicates there is a question but it is not urgent, and a red cup indicates an urgent need for help.

## Why This Works

- **Research base (teacher recommendation).** I have used variations of three cups in my classes at many different grade levels. Sometimes they are colored cards to flip on the desktop. Sometimes I have students hold up fingers to assess their level of understanding (e.g., "Show me one through five fingers—five means you are an expert, one means you are completely lost") to provide me with an immediate sense of who needs more information and to provide the students with an opportunity to assess themselves.

- **Student involvement.** This strategy provides students with a simple but effective way to reflect on their own performance and needs.

- **Reasonable use.** Cups or cards are inexpensive, durable, and reusable. Scaffolding students in effective self-evaluation may take some modeling and practice.

- **Expectations maintained.** This strategy allows students to determine their level of understanding, independence, and frustration with a task or concept.

- **Equity and universality.** All students should have materials that meet their needs and they are able to use to signal for help.

→ IF . . . THEN ←

If this strategy is used to provide an alternative means for students to express a need for assistance, then this can also be a strategy for **Output.**

OUTPUT

# A Living Resource

# REFLECTIONS FOR ADDITIONAL STRATEGIES

This book is intended to be a live, dynamic, growing, ever-changing resource. The strategies in this book are a good start to becoming an inclusive teacher who universally designs curriculum and classrooms for learning. It is important to remember, however, that it is just that—a start. The strategies in this book cannot possibly be comprehensive. There are thousands of ideas out there, perhaps even millions. That said, the strategies in this book are great examples of ways to ensure full citizenship of all students in the classroom. They embody UDL, UbD, DI, and brain-based research. They are culturally responsive and send a message that the learning community is for *everyone*. If anyone can have access to a strategy, everyone should have access to it.

The strategies here can help you start on your own process of creating a classroom that is for everyone. I hope that there are ideas here that are new to you. Perhaps others are familiar but long forgotten, or you were not aware of the research behind them or the variety of ways they can be implemented. I hope you read some of the strategies and thought, "I already do that!" If that is the case, thank you for being a creative, inclusive teacher. I hope you will send me new ideas that I have not learned yet.

To continue building a learning community for everyone, new strategies and resources should be added to this book over time, through experience. To add strategies in keeping with the conceptual framework of this book, be sure to consider the following reflection questions:

## What Is the Research Base or Teacher-Tested Resource for the Strategy?

Many strategies are tried in the classroom because they seem cute or fun. This is fine as long as there is also a foundation for their effectiveness. The strategies in this book are founded on research and/or have been teacher tested for effectiveness. When you consider a new strategy, be aware of where it comes from and what it is based on.

## Does the Strategy Offer Opportunity for Students to Be Involved in its Development, Implementation, and/or Evaluation?

In order for students to become independent self-advocates, they need as many opportunities as possible to be involved in their learning and reflect on the effectiveness of various strategies. They also need opportunities to reflect on their own experiences. The strategies in this book offer ways that students can be as independent as possible while still benefiting from the guidance and expertise of the teacher. When you add a strategy, be sure to plan how students will eventually take over its implementation and how students will think about its value.

## Is the Strategy Reasonable to Implement in the Classroom?

To be reasonable, the strategy should not require extensive training, significant cost, or customized installation. Some strategies in this book are free; others cost money to purchase materials or to implement. When you consider adding a new strategy, consider the cost–benefit ratio. Perhaps a very effective idea that will benefit many students is worth the expense.

## Does the Strategy Maintain High Expectations for All Students?

All students should be expected to learn equitable (if not identical) knowledge and skills. Strategies should not replace or water down an objective. They should provide alternative ways to achieve it. The strategies in this book do not excuse students from achieving new skills; they support them toward even greater achievements. When you add a strategy, ask yourself whether all students will be meeting the same goal or if some will be held to a higher or lower standard than others. The expectation is that all students are capable of achieving the essential learning, albeit in different ways and at different rates. If you do not believe all students are capable of doing that, you are holding them back yourself.

## Do All Members of the Learning Community Have Equitable Access to and Universal Use of the Strategy?

Everyone in the community should have an opportunity to try and evaluate the strategy for him- or herself. The strategies, materials, and choices presented in this book are meant to be available for all, not just a select few. Majority does not rule; universality rules. Even if only one student in the classroom benefits from the strategy, it still needs to be available at all times and remain a choice for others to try again in the future. Developing students are always changing, so the number who benefit from the option will always be changing.

In the following sections, you will find many helpful resources (some cited in previous sections). There are books that delve into theoretical foundations of education and books that describe more strategies. There are web sites for products, services, agencies, and support groups. Remember that not everything from all of the resources will work for your students. Digest the ideas and see if they fit the five criteria in the questions just discussed. Let the search begin!

## THEORY BOOKS

Brightman, A. (2008). *Disabilityland*. New York, NY: SelectBooks.

Cowhey, M. (2006). *Black ants and Buddhists: Thinking critically and teaching differently in the primary grades*. Portland, ME: Stenhouse Publishers.

Delpit, L. (2006). *Other people's children: Cultural conflict in the classroom*. New York, NY: The New Press.

Peterson, J.M., & Hittie, M.M. (2010). *Inclusive teaching: The journey towards effective schools for all learners* (2nd ed.). Boston, MA: Pearson.

Rethinking Schools. (2004). *Rethinking our classrooms: Teaching for equity and justice* (Vol. II). Milwaukee, WI: Author.

Rethinking Schools. (2007). *Rethinking our classrooms: Teaching for equity and justice* (Vol. I, 2nd ed.). Milwaukee, WI: Author.

Schniedewind, N., & Davidson, E. (2006). *Open minds to equality: A sourcebook of learning activities to affirm diversity and promote equity* (3rd ed.). Milwaukee, WI: Rethinking Schools.

Sousa, D.A., & Tomlinson, C.A. (2011). *Differentiation and the brain: How neuroscience supports the learner-friendly classroom*. Bloomington, IN: Solution Tree Press.

## STRATEGY BOOKS AND MATERIALS

Buron, K.D. (2007). *A 5 is against the law: Social boundaries: Straight up! An honest guide for teens and young adults.* Shawnee Mission, KS: Autism Asperger Publishing.

Buron, K.D., & Curtis, M. (2012). *The incredible 5-point scale: Assisting students in understanding social situations and controlling their emotional responses* (2nd ed.). Shawnee Mission, KS: Autism Asperger Publishing.

Columba, L., & Lieberman, L. (2011). *Promoting language through physical education: Using sign language and Spanish to engage everyone.* Champaign, IL: Human Kinetics.

Golden, C. (2012). *The special educator's toolkit: Everything you need to organize, manage, and monitor your classroom.* Baltimore, MD: Paul H. Brookes Publishing Co.

Kluth, P., & Danaher, S. (2010). *From tutor scripts to talking sticks: 100 ways to differentiate instruction in K–12 inclusive classrooms.* Baltimore, MD: Paul H. Brookes Publishing Co.

Kluth, P., & Danaher, S. (2014). *From text maps to memory caps: 100 more ways to differentiate instruction in K–12 classrooms.* Baltimore, MD: Paul H. Brookes Publishing Co.

Kriete, R. (2002). *The morning meeting book.* Turner Falls, MA: The Northeast Foundation for Children.

Lavoie, R. (2005). *It's so much work to be your friend: Helping the child with learning disabilities find social success.* New York, NY: Touchstone.

Lieberman, L., & Houston-Wilson, C. (2009). *Strategies for inclusion: A handbook for physical educators* (2nd ed.). Champaign, IL: Human Kinetics.

Mooney, J., & Cole, D. (2000). *Learning outside the lines: Two Ivy League students with learning disabilities and ADHD give you the tools for academic success and educational revolution.* New York, NY: Fireside.

Nelson, J., Lott, L., & Glenn, S. (2000). *Positive discipline in the classroom: Developing mutual respect, cooperation, and responsibility in your classroom.* New York, NY: Three Rivers Press.

Peterson, J.M., & Hittie, M.M. (2010). *Inclusive teaching: The journey towards effective schools for all learners.* Boston, MA: Pearson.

Rutherford, P. (2008). *Instruction for all students* (2nd ed.). Alexandria, VA: Just ASK Publications.

Rutherford, P. (2009a). *Strategies in action: A collection of classroom applications* (Vol. I). Alexandria, VA: Just ASK Publications.

Rutherford, P. (2009b). *Why didn't I learn this in college?* (2nd ed.). Alexandria, VA: Just ASK Publications.

Rutherford, P. (2010). *Meeting the needs of diverse learners.* Alexandria, VA: Just ASK Publications.

Rutherford, P. (2011). *Strategies in action: Volume II: Applications in today's diverse classrooms.* Alexandria, VA: Just ASK Publications.

Rutherford, P. (2012). *Active learning and engagement strategies: Teaching and learning in the 21st century.* Alexandria, VA: Just ASK Publications.

Rutherford, P., Kaylor, B., Kwit, H.C., & McVicker, J. (2011). *Creating a culture for learning.* Alexandria, VA: Just ASK Publications.

Schoolhouse Rock: Disney (Executive Producer). (2002). *Schoolhouse Rock, Special 30th anniversary edition* [DVD]. New York, NY: Buena Vista Home Entertainment.

Smith, T.B. (2002). *Guidelines: Practical tips for working and socializing with deaf-blind people.* Burtonsville, MD: Sign Media.

Thoma, C.A., Bartholomew, C.C., & Scott, L.A. (2009). *Universal design for transition: A roadmap for planning and instruction.* Baltimore, MD: Paul H. Brookes Publishing Co.

Wong, H.K., & Wong, R.T. (1998). *The first days of school: How to be an effective teacher.* Mountain View, CA: Harry K. Wong Publications.

Wormeli, R. (2001). *Meet in the middle: Becoming an accomplished middle-level teacher.* Portland, ME: Stenhouse Publishers.

Wormeli, R. (2003). *Day one and beyond: Practical matters for new middle-level teachers.* Portland, ME: Stenhouse Publishers.

Wormeli, R. (2006). *Fair isn't always equal: Assessing and grading in the differentiated classroom.* Portland, ME: Stenhouse Publishers.

Wormeli, R. (2007). *Differentiation: From planning to practice, grades 6–12.* Portland, ME: Stenhouse Publishers.

Wormeli, R. (2009). *Metaphors and analogies: Power tools for teaching any subject.* Portland, ME: Stenhouse Publishers.

## FIRST-HAND NARRATIVES

Giordano, K., & Giordano, M. (2012). *A family's quest for rhythm: Living with Tourette, ADD, OCD and challenging behaviors.* Available from http://www.afamilysquest.com.

Goddard, P., & Goddard, D. (2012). *I am intelligent: From heartbreak to healing—A mother and daughter's journey through autism.* Guilford, CT: Skirt! Books.

Johnson, H.M. (2005). *Too late to die young: Nearly true tales from a life.* New York, NY: Picador.

Kingsley, J., & Levitz, M. (1994). *Count us in: Growing up with Down syndrome.* Orlando, FL: Harvest.

Mooney, J. (2007). *The short bus: A journey beyond normal.* New York, NY: Henry Holt & Co.

## WEB SITES

AbleNet (http://www.ablenetinc.com/Assistive-Technology/Computer-Access)

This site provides educational and technical solutions for children and adults with disabilities. The company offers a complete line of communication aids for nonverbal learners, access aids for learners of all ages and situations, and special education classroom curricula. Their products are used in homes, clinics, and classrooms worldwide.

American Association of the Deaf-Blind (AADB; http://www.aadb.org)

> AADB is a national nonprofit organization whose members consist of deaf-blind people from diverse backgrounds, as well as family members, professionals, interpreters, and other interested supporters. *Deaf-blind* includes all types and degrees of dual vision and hearing loss.

American Speech-Language-Hearing Association (ASHA; http://www.asha.org)

> ASHA is the national professional, scientific, and credentialing association for audiologists; speech-language pathologists; speech, language, and hearing scientists; audiology and speech-language pathology support personnel; and students.

Association for Comprehensive Neurotherapy (ACN; http://www.latitudes.org)

> ACN is a nonprofit organization dedicated to exploring advanced and alternative nontoxic treatments for anxiety, autism, attention-deficit/hyperactivity disorder, depression, obsessive compulsive disorder, tics and Tourette syndrome, and learning disabilities.

The Audio Description Project (http://www.acb.org/adp/accessibility.html)

> This web site is an initiative of the American Council of the Blind. It is designed to conform with standard coding conventions that make everything on the site accessible to individuals who are blind and use screen readers to read web site content.

AudioBooks (http://www.audiobooks.com)

> This free e-book service offers more than 25,000 titles.

Bag Books (http://www.bagbooks.org)

> Bag Books is a charity out of the United Kingdom that provides tactile and multisensory books to people with learning disabilities.

Boardmaker (http://www.mayer-johnson.com/boardmaker-software)

> Boardmaker software is used to create print materials, such as communication boards, with Picture Communication Symbols (PCS) and other pictures and graphics.

Bookshare (https://www.bookshare.org)

> This site is an accessible online library for people with print disabilities.

Brain Gym (http://www.braingym.org)

> Brain Gym is a movement-based educational model.

BrainPOP (http://www.brainpop.com)

> This site offers animated content in science, social studies, English, math, engineering and tech, health, and arts and music.

Carol Ann Tomlinson's web site (http://www.caroltomlinson.com)

> Carol Ann Tomlinson is a teacher, teacher educator, and author of many books, articles and professional development materials about differentiated instruction and understanding by design.

CAST Learning Tools (http://www.cast.org/learningtools/index.html)

> CAST provides a library of online learning tools for all areas.

CAST UDL Book Builder (http://bookbuilder.cast.org)

> This site helps teachers create, share, and publish digital books for diverse learners.

Castle Learning Online (https://www.castlelearning.com/review/castlesoftware/home.aspx)

> Castle Learning is a K–12 resource that provides core testing content using a variety of formats. It provides instant grading, detailed assessment reports, and instructional feedback and aligns with state and Common Core State Standards.

Center for Inclusive Design and Environmental Access (http://idea.ap.buffalo.edu)

> This organization helps make environments and products safer, healthier, and more usable for individuals with disabilities.

Center for Universal Design (CUD; http://www.ncsu.edu/ncsu/design/cud/index.htm)

> This national information, technical assistance, and research center evaluates, develops, and promotes accessible and universal design in housing, commercial and public facilities, outdoor environments, and products.

Children and Adults with Attention-Deficit/Hyperactivity Disorder (CHADD; http://www.chadd.org)

> CHADD is a membership organization for individuals with ADHD and their parents. It produces the bi-monthly *Attention* magazine (for members) and sponsors an annual conference.

Classroom Seating Solutions (http://classroomseatingsolutions.com)

> This site provides alternate seating options for students who may not learn best using traditional desks.

Drum Echoes (http://www.drumechoes.org)

> This organization offers custom drum circles to help students de-stress, relax, and get in tune with their bodies' natural rhythms.

edHelper.com (http://edhelper.com/teachers/graphic_organizers.htm)

> This site provides a library of printable graphic organizers.

EdTech Solutions (http://teachingeverystudent.blogspot.com/2007/06/free-technology-toolkit-for-udl-in-all.html)

> This site provides free UDL resources.

Educational Learning Games (http://www.educationallearninggames.com)

> This site provides a large selection of educational board and card games.

Education Oasis (http://www.educationoasis.com/curriculum/graphic_organizers.htm)

> This site offers graphic organizers in PDF form. Some of the graphic organizers may be filled out and then printed.

Edutopia (http://www.edutopia.org/brain-based-learning-research-resources)

This site provides a list of resources, articles, videos, and links for exploring the connection between education and neuroscience.

EnableMart (http://www.enablemart.com/learning-and-instruction/toys-and-games/accessible-board-games)

EnableMart is an online store for adapted games and toys.

Fun and Function (http://www.funandfunction.com)

This site provides occupational therapy toys for children.

The Gray Center (https://www.thegraycenter.org/social-stories/carol-gray)

This nonprofit organization cultivates the strengths of individuals with autism and those who interact with them, and globally promotes social understanding.

Holt Interactive Graphic Organizers (http://my.hrw.com/nsmedia/intgos/html/igo.htm)

This site provides a library of printable graphic organizers.

Interpretype (http://www.interpretype.com)

Interpretype provides communication tools that enable communication between deaf and hearing individuals, as well as translated conversations from English to any of 240 foreign languages.

Intervention Central (http://www.interventioncentral.org)

On this web site, teachers can search a database of research-based instructional and behavioral RTI strategies.

iSmartboard (http://www.ismartboard.com)

This site provides SMART board activities and lessons for reading and writing English language arts, math, science, social studies, art, health and physical education, library, music, foreign language, and holidays.

Kagan Publishing & Professional Development (http://www.kaganonline.com)

Kagan offers workshops and products on active student learning, including cooperative learning, brain-friendly instruction, multiple intelligences, DI, the Win-Win Discipline, and classroom management.

Laurie Westphal's series of *Differentiating Instruction with Menus* books from Prufrock Press (http://www.prufrock.com/cw_contributorinfo.aspx?ContribID=257&Name=Laurie+E.+Westphal)

These books discuss everything teachers need to create a student-centered learning environment based on choice.

Learning Resources (http://www.learningresources.com)

Learning Resources manufactures innovative, hands-on educational products.

Learning, Sight, and Sound (LS&S; http://www.lssproducts.com)

>   LS&S specializes in products for individuals who are blind, have visual impairments, are deaf, or are hard of hearing.

Lives In The Balance (http://www.livesinthebalance.org)

>   This nonprofit organization advocates on behalf of children with behavioral challenges and their parents, teachers, and other caregivers.

Livescribe (http://www.livescribe.com/en-us)

>   This company manufactures low-cost mobile computing platforms that enhance productivity, learning, communication, and self-expression through the use of a pen and paper. The Echo and Pulse smartpens record and link audio to handwriting.

Mind Tools (http://www.mindtools.com/index.html)

>   This site provides resources on leadership, team management, problem-solving, personal productivity, and team-working skills.

Minecraft (http://minecraft.net)

>   Minecraft is a game about breaking and placing blocks in order to build structures and landscapes. It promotes planning, organization, material management, dexterity, and cooperation. The game can be played individually or collaboratively online and is available for multiple platforms.

National Center on Accessible Instructional Materials (http://aim.cast.org/)

>   This site serves as a resource to educators, parents, publishers, conversion houses, accessible media producers, and others interested in learning more about and implementing accessible instructional materials and the National Instructional Materials Accessibility Standard.

NaturalReader (http://www.naturalreaders.com)

>   This easy-to-use text-to-speech software can read text from Microsoft Word files, web pages, PDF files, and e-mails. NaturalReader can also convert any written text into audio files.

Notability (https://itunes.apple.com/us/app/notability-take-notes-annotate/id360593530?mt=8)

>   This app integrates handwriting, PDF annotation, typing, recording, and organizing. Users can compile their notes in one place.

Paula Kluth's web site (http://www.paulakluth.com)

>   Dr. Paula Kluth is a consultant, author, advocate, and independent scholar who works with teachers and families to provide inclusive opportunities for students with disabilities.

PBS Kids Interactive Whiteboard Games (http://pbskids.org/whiteboard)

>   This site provides a collection of interactive whiteboard games for educators.

Perkins School for the Blind (http://www.perkins.org)

> This school provides education and services for children and adults who are blind, are deafblind, or have a visual impairment, with or without other disabilities.

Picture Communication Symbols (http://www.mayer-johnson.com/category/symbols-and-photos)

> This site offers a wide range of symbol and photo collections and software that allows teachers to create effective communication and educational supports for learners with special needs.

Powtoon (http://www.powtoon.com)

> This site provides animation tools to create professional-looking videos and presentations.

Prezi (http://prezi.com)

> This presentation tool helps teachers organize and share their ideas.

Princeton Review (http://www.princetonreview.com/free-online-practice-tests.aspx)

> This site provides free online practice tests for the ACT, GRE, and so forth. It provides a detailed score report that analyzes strengths and weaknesses.

Readingprof.com (http://www.readingprof.com/papers.html)

> The site offers a link to "Brain-Friendly Humor in the Classroom," which shares ideas for integrating humor into lessons and class procedures.

Rethinking Schools (http://www.rethinkingschools.org)

> Rethinking Schools is a nonprofit, independent publisher of educational materials with a strong emphasis on issues of equity and social justice.

Rick Lavoie's web site (http://www.ricklavoie.com)

> This site provides information and inspiration for parents and teachers of children with learning disabilities.

Rochester Institute of Technology MindGamers (http://www.rit.edu/research/biox_story.php?id=105)

> This site explains how gaming technology can provide novel ways to treat individuals with mental health issues. Professors at Rochester Institute of Technology are exploring the use of virtual reality in therapy.

Scholastic Interactive Whiteboard Lessons (http://www.scholastic.com/smarttech/teachers.htm)

> This site is a place for educators to share interactive resources to inspire each other and student learning. It offers free downloadable standards-correlated digital lessons, assessments, and copyright-cleared content.

School Specialty (http://www.schoolspecialty.com)

> This site provides solutions focused on helping educators help students succeed.

Signed Stories (http://www.signedstories.com)

> This site helps improve the literacy of deaf children. It provides useful advice and guidance for the parents, caregivers, and teachers of deaf children, and for the deaf parents of hearing children.

Skype (http://www.skype.com/en)

> Skype allows teachers to make free Internet calls, send instant messages, and video chat with distant teachers, classrooms, or subject matter experts as part of a lesson.

SlideRocket (http://www.sliderocket.com)

> This site helps teachers create presentations.

Smart Moves (http://www.smartmovespointer.com)

> The SmartMoves pointer helps students manipulate images on an interactive whiteboard. Its design is helpful for young children and those who cannot reach the top of the whiteboard.

Tai Chi for Kids (http://www.taichiforkids.com)

> This educational activity improves balance, concentration, flexibility, focus, attention, and learning.

Tangle Creations (http://www.tanglecreations.com)

> Tangle Toys are twistable therapy devices that are both therapeutic and calming.

TASH (http://www.tash.org)

> TASH is an international organization that advocates for human rights and inclusion for people with significant disabilities and support needs. TASH works to advance inclusive communities through advocacy; research; professional development; policy; and information and resources for parents, families, and self-advocates.

TeacherVision (http://www.teachervision.fen.com/graphic-organizers/printable/6293.html)

> This site provides ready-to-use graphic organizers that facilitate understanding of key concepts by allowing students to visually identify key points and ideas. It offers graphic organizers for reading, science, writing, math, and general use as well as blank printable templates.

Teaching Tolerance (http://www.tolerance.org)

> This site provides news, discussion, and support for educators who care about diversity, equal opportunity, and respect for differences in schools.

Texas School for the Blind and Visually Impaired (TSBVI; http://www.tsbvi.edu)

> TSBVI is a public school in Texas that provides specialized and intense services to students with visual impairments, including those with additional disabilities.

Therapy Fun Zone (http://therapyfunzone.com/blog/ot/fine-motor-skills)

> This site provides ideas for making occupational and physical therapy fun for both the student and the therapist.

Therapy Shoppe (http://www.therapyshoppe.com)

> The Therapy Shoppe specializes in sensory-integration products, toys for children with special needs, oral motor tools, and occupational therapy supplies.

They Might Be Giants (http://www.theymightbegiants.com)

> They Might Be Giants is a band from Brooklyn, New York, founded by John Flansburgh and John Linnell. Children love their unique music.

Thinking Reader by Tom Snyder Productions (http://www.tomsnyder.com/products/product.asp?sku=THITHI)

> This research-validated program builds reading comprehension skills for students reading below grade level.

Thinkport (http://www.thinkport.org/technology/template.tp)

> Thinkport offers a collection of preformatted graphic organizers to integrate into activities and lesson plans or use by themselves.

TumbleBookCloud (http://www.tumblebookcloud.com)

> This site provides an online collection of e-books and read-along chapter books, graphic novels, educational videos, and audio books. All books are available with unlimited access from any device with an Internet connection.

Twist 'N Write pencil (http://www.drawyourworld.com/twist-n-write)

> This wishbone-shaped mechanical pencil helps children position their fingers in the tripod grasp.

UDL Strategies (https://udlstrategies.wikispaces.com/Multiple+Means+of+Engagement)

> This site provides a library of online blogs, wikis, and resources.

VisualBee presentation software (http://www.visualbee.com/free/free-presentation-software.html)

> This software helps teachers compile lesson content in an effective PowerPoint presentation.

VizZle (http://www.monarchteachtech.com/vizzle)

> VizZle provides online software for teaching visual learners.

Windows Speech Recognition (http://windows.microsoft.com/en-us/windows7/dictate-text-using-speech-recognition)

> This site allows users to dictate text to a computer, for example, to fill out online forms or dictate a letter to a word-processing program.

WordTalk (http://www.wordtalk.org.uk/Home)

> This site provides a free text-to-speech plug-in.

Yoga 4 Classrooms (http://www.yoga4classrooms.com)

> This program facilitates students' physical, mental, emotional, and social-personal growth. It is evidence based and low cost.

YouTube (http://www.youtube.com)

This site allows users to watch and share originally created videos and provides a forum for users to connect.

# References

American Speech-Language-Hearing Association. (2013). *Augmentative and alternative communication (AAC)*. Retrieved from http://www.asha.org/public/speech/disorders/AAC/

Brewer, C.B. (1995). *Music and learning: Integrating music in the classroom*. Retrieved from The Johns Hopkins School of Education web site: http://education.jhu.edu/PD/newhorizons/strategies/topics/Arts%20in%20Education/brewer.htm

Brown, C. (2010). *Environmental checklist for developing independence*. Retrieved from http://www.tsbvi.edu/orientation-a-mobility/1969-environmental-checklist-for-developing-independence?device=desktop

Buron, K.D., & Curtis, M. (2012). *The incredible 5-point scale: Assisting students in understanding social situations and controlling their emotional responses* (2nd ed.). Shawnee Mission, KS: Autism Asperger Publishing.

Candler, L. (2000). *Science buddies: Cooperative science activities*. San Clemente, CA: Kagan Cooperative Learning.

CAST. (2011). *Universal Design for Learning Guidelines version 2.0*. Wakefield, MA: Author.

CAST. (2012). *Chapter 4: Developing reading engagement*. Retrieved from http://www.cast.org/library/books/ltr/chapter4.html

Chatterton, S., & Butler, S. (1994). The development of communication skills through drama. *Down Syndrome Research and Practice, 2*(2), 83–84.

Chorzempa, B.F., & Lapidus, L. (2009). "To find yourself, think for yourself": Using Socratic discussions in inclusive classrooms. *TEACHING Exceptional Children, 41*(3), 54–59.

Clark, J., & Nordness, P. (2007, July). *Enhancing emergent literacy skills with SMART Board interactive whiteboard technology*. Retrieved from http://downloads01.smarttech.com/media/sitecore/en/pdf/research_library/k-12/enhancing%20emergent_literacy_skills_with_smart_board_interactive_whiteboard.pdf

Cohen, M.J., & Sloan, D.L. (2007). *Visual supports for people with autism: A guide for parents and professionals*. Bethesda, MD: Woodbine House.

College Board. (2013). *Standardized Achievement Tests*. Retrieved from http://sat.collegeboard.org/home

Connolly, A.J. (2007). *Key math-2 diagnostic assessment*. San Antonio, TX: Pearson.

Cooley, T. (2013). *Fine motor skills*. Retrieved from http://therapyfunzone.com/blog/ot/fine-motor-skills/

Cooper-Kahn, J., & Dietzel, L.C. (2008). *Late, lost, and unprepared: A parent's guide to helping children with executive functioning*. Bethesda, MD: Woodbine House.

Dawson, P., & Guare, R. (2004). *Executive skills in children and adolescents: A practical guide to assessment and intervention*. New York, NY: The Guilford Press.

Dendy, C.A.Z. (2008). *Executive function: "What is it anyway?"* Retrieved from http://www.chrisdendy.com/executive.htm

Doyle, M.B., & Giangreco, M.F. (2009). Making presentation software accessible to high school students with intellectual disabilities. *TEACHING Exceptional Children, 41*(3), 24–31.

Dunn, R., Dunn, K., & Price, G.E. (1984). *Learning style inventory*. Lawrence, KS: Price Systems.

Edens, K.M., & Potter, E. (2003). Using descriptive drawings as a conceptual change strategy in elementary science. *School Science and Mathematics, 103*(3), 135–144.

Education Northwest. (2013). *6+1 trait writing prompts*. Retrieved from http://educationnorthwest.org/resource/514

Educational Testing Service. (2005). *Reducing test anxiety: A guide for Praxis test takers*. Retrieved from http://www.ets.org/s/praxis/pdf/reducing_test_anxiety.pdf

Ellis, M. (2009). *Skype in the classroom*. Retrieved from http://www.ecu.edu/cs-itcs/thinkin/upload/Ellis.pdf

Engelbrecht, K. (2003). *The impact of color on learning*. Retrieved from http://sdpl.coe.uga.edu/HTML/W305.pdf

Gargiulo, R.M., & Metcalf, D. (2010). *Teaching in today's inclusive classroom: A universal design for learning approach*. Belmont, CA: Wadsworth Cengage Learning.

Gay, G. (2002). Preparing for culturally-responsive teaching. *Journal of Teacher Education, 53*(2), 106–116.

Gay, G. (2010). *Culturally responsive teaching: Theory, research, and practice* (2nd ed.). New York, NY: Teachers College Press.

Golden, C. (2012). *The special educator's toolkit: Everything you need to organize, manage, and monitor your classroom.* Baltimore, MD: Paul H. Brookes Publishing Co.

Gray, C. (2010). *The new social story book.* Austin, TX: Future Horizons.

Hannaford, C. (2005). *Smart moves: Why learning is not all in your head.* Salt Lake City, UT: Great River Books.

Henderson, J.G., Hutchison, J., & Newman, C. (1998). Maxine Greene and the present/future democratization of curriculum. In W.F. Pinar (Ed.), *The passionate mind of Maxine Greene: "I am...not yet"* (pp. 189–211). Bristol, PA: Falmer Press.

Higgins, E.L., & Raskind, M.H. (2005). The compensatory effectiveness of the Quicktionary Reading Pen II on the reading comprehension of students with learning disabilities. *Journal of Special Education Technology, 20*(1). Retrieved from http://frostig.org/wp-content/uploads/2012/02/Reading-Pen-JSET.pdf

Higher Education Opportunity Act of 2008, PL 110-315, 20 U.S.C. §§1001 *et seq.*

Hobbs, R. (2007, March 17). *Using audio books to promote critical listening skills.* Presentation at the annual meeting of the International Reading Association, Toronto, Canada.

Honey, P., & Mumford, A. (2006). *The learning styles questionnaire, 80 items version.* Maidenhead, UK: Peter Honey Publications.

Individuals with Disabilities Education Improvement Act (IDEA) of 2004, PL 108-446, 20 U.S.C. §§ 1400 *et seq.*

Jacobs, S., Rice, R., & Sugarman, L. (2012, October). *Creating MindGamers: Building communication, design and development process with clinicians, game faculty and students.* Meaningful Play Conference Proceedings 2012, East Lansing, Michigan.

Jago, E., & Tanner, K. (1999). *Influence of the school facility on student achievement.* Retrieved from http://sdpl.coe.uga.edu/researchabstracts/visual.html

Johnson, C.S., & Thomas, A.T. (2009). Caring as classroom practice. *Social Studies and the Young Learner, 22*(1), 8–11.

Kagan, S. (2008, Summer). Kagan structures simply put. *Kagan Online Magazine.* Retrieved from http://www.kaganonline.com/free_articles/dr_spencer_kagan/ASK38.php

Kamps, D.M. (2002). Preventing problems by improving behavior. In B. Algozzine & P. Kay (Eds.), *Preventing problem behaviors: A handbook of successful prevention strategies* (pp. 11–36). Thousand Oaks, CA: Corwin Press.

Kaufman, C. (2010). *Executive function in the classroom: Practical strategies for improving performance and enhancing skills for all students.* Baltimore, MD: Paul H. Brookes Publishing Co.

Kilbourne, J. (2009, February). Sharpening the mind through movement: Using exercise balls in a university lecture class. *The Chronicle of Kinesiology and Physical Education in Higher Education.*

Kliewer, C. (1998). *Schooling children with Down syndrome: Toward an understanding of possibility.* New York, NY: Teachers College Press.

Kluth, P., & Danaher, S. (2010). *From tutor scripts to talking sticks: 100 ways to differentiate instruction in K–12 inclusive classrooms.* Baltimore, MD: Paul H. Brookes Publishing Co.

Kohn, A. (2006). *The homework myth: Why our kids get too much of a bad thing.* Philadelphia, PA: De Capo Press.

Kolb, D. (1984). *Experiential learning: Experience as the source of learning and development.* Englewood Cliffs, NJ: Prentice-Hall.

Kriete, R. (2002). *The morning meeting book.* Turner Falls, MA: The Northeast Foundation for Children.

Kroeger, S.D., Burton, C., & Preston, C. (2009). Integrating evidence-based practices in middle school learning. *TEACHING Exceptional Children, 41*(3), 6–15.

Kunc, N. (2013). Untitled presentation at 2013 TASH conference, Long Beach, CA.

Lavoie, R. (2005a). *It's so much work to be your friend: Helping the child with learning disabilities find social success.* New York, NY: Touchstone.

Lavoie, R. (2005b). *Social skill autopsies: A strategy to promote and develop social competencies.* Retrieved from http://www.ldonline.org/article/14910/

Maslow, A.H., Frager, R.D., & Fadiman, J. (1987). *Motivation and personality* (3rd ed.). Upper Saddle River, NJ: Pearson Education.

McGregor, T. (2007). *Comprehension connections: Bridges to strategic reading.* Portsmouth, NH: Heinemann.

McTighe, J., & Wiggins, G. (1999). *The understanding by design handbook.* Alexandria, VA: Association for Supervision and Curriculum Development.

Meyer, B., Haywood, N., Sachdev, D., & Faraday S. (2008). *Independent learning literature review.* Nottingham, England: Department for Children Schools and Family.

Miller, M. (2006). Where they are: Working with marginalized students. *Educational Leadership, 63*(5), 50–54.

Morrison, G., & Cosden, M. (1997). Risk, resilience, and adjustment of individuals with learning disabilities. *Learning Disability Quarterly, 20,* 43–60.

National Assessment of Educational Progress. (2011). *The nation's report card.* Retrieved from http://nationsreportcard.gov/

National Center for Learning Disabilities. (2012). *What is dysgraphia?* Retrieved from http://www.ncld.org/types-learning-disabilities/dysgraphia/what-is-dysgraphia

National Center on Universal Design for Learning. (2011). *The three principles of UDL.* Retrieved from http://www.udlcenter.org/aboutudl/whatisudl/3principles

National Research Council. (2000). *How people learn: Brain, mind, experience, and school.* Washington, DC: The National Academies Press.

Nelson, J., Lott, L., & Glenn, S. (2000). *Positive discipline in the classroom: Developing mutual respect, cooperation, and responsibility in your classroom* (3rd ed.). New York, NY: Three Rivers Press.

Nelson, L.L. (2014). *Design and deliver: Planning and teaching using universal design for learning.* Baltimore, MD: Paul H. Brookes Publishing Co.

New York State Education Department. (2013). *New York State Regents examinations.* Retrieved from http://www.nysl.nysed.gov/regentsexams.htm

North Carolina State University (NCSU). (1997). *The principles of universal design.* Retrieved from http://www.ncsu.edu/ncsu/design/cud/about_ud/udprinciplestext.htm

Packer, L.E. (2010). *Overview of executive dysfunction.* Retrieved from http://www.schoolbehavior.com/disorders/executive-dysfuntion/overview-of-executive-dysfunction/

Palinscar, A.S., & Brown, A.L. (1984). Reciprocal teaching of comprehension-fostering and comprehension-monitoring activities. *Cognition and Instruction, 2,* 117–175.

Piaget, J. (1952). *The origin of intelligence in children.* Madison, CT: International Universities Press.

Pisha, B., & Coyne, P. (2001). Smart from the start: The promise of universal design for learning. *Remedial and Special Education, 22*(197). Retrieved from http://rse.sagepub.com/content/22/4/197

Rapp, W.H. (1997). *I hear, and I forget; I see, and I remember; I do, and I understand: An exploration of children's museums as successful learning environments for students with and without disabilities.* Unpublished dissertation, Department of Counseling, Educational Psychology and Special Education, Michigan State University, East Lansing.

Rapp, W.H. (2009). Avoiding math taboos: Effective math strategies for visual-spatial learners. *TEACHING Exceptional Children Plus, 6*(2), 1–12.

Rapp, W., & Arndt, K.L. (2012). *Teaching everyone: An introduction to inclusive education.* Baltimore, MD: Paul H. Brookes Publishing Co.

Rasinski, T., Flexer, C., & Szypulski, T. (2006). *The sound of learning: Why self-amplification matters.* Minneapolis, MN: Harebrain.

Rehabilitation Act of 1973, PL 93-112, U.S.C. §§ 504 *et seq.*

Riener, C., & Willingham, D. (2010, September-October). *The myth of learning styles.* Retrieved from http://www.changemag.org/Archives/Back%20Issues/September-October%202010

Rodis, P., Garrod, A., & Boscardin, M.L. (2001). *Learning disabilities and life stories.* Boston, MA: Pearson.

Roid, G.H. (2003). *Stanford-Binet Intelligence Scales* (SB5; 5th ed.). Rolling Meadows, IL: Riverside Publishing.

Rolheiser, C., & Ross, J.A. (n.d.). *Student self-evaluation: What research says and what practice shows.* Retrieved from http://www.cdl.org/resource-library/articles/self_eval.php?type=subject&id=4

Rose, D.H., & Meyer, A. (2002). *Teaching every student in the digital age: Universal design for learning.* Alexandria, VA: Association for Supervision and Curriculum Development.

Rutherford, P. (2002). *Why didn't I learn this in college? Teaching and learning in the 21st century.* Alexandria, VA: Just ASK.

Salend, S. (2009). Using technology to create and administer accessible tests. *TEACHING Exceptional Children, 41*(3), 40–51.

Schilling, D.L., Washington, K., Billingsley, F.F., & Deitz, J. (2003). Classroom seating for children with attention deficit hyperactivity disorder: Therapy balls versus chairs. *American Journal of Occupational Therapy, 57*(5). Retrieved from http://www.ateachabout.com/pdf/ClassroomSeatingUsingBalls.pdf

Sharp, L.A. (2012). *Stealth learning: Unexpected learning opportunities through games.* Retrieved from http://www.gcu.edu/Academics/Journal-of-Instructional-Research/-Unexpected-Learning-Opportunities-Through-Games-.php

Shepard, R.J. (1997). Curricular physical activity and academic performance. *Pediatric Exercise Science, 9*(2), 113–126.

Silverman, L.K. (2002). *Upside-down brilliance: The visual-spatial learner.* Denver, CO: DeLeon Publishing.

Smith, A. (2010). Effects of chewing gum on cognitive function, mood and physiology in stressed and non-stressed volunteers. *Nutritional Neuroscience, 13*(1), 7–16.

Smith, A.J., & Pecore, J. (2008). Students experience SMART board through constructivist values. In L.P. McCoy (Ed.), *Studies in teaching: 2008 Research digest research projects presented at annual research forum* (pp. 169–174). Winston-Salem, NC: Wake Forest University Department of Education.

Somekh, B., Haldene, M., Jones, K., Lewin, C., Steadman, S., Scrimshaw, P.,...Woodrow, D. (2007). *Evaluation of the primary schools whiteboard expansion project—summary report: Report to the Department for Children, Schools, and Families.* Retrieved from http://downloads01.smarttech.com/media/research/international_research/uk/becta_executive_expansion_summary.pdf

Southern Regional Educational Board. (2012, February). *Creating a culture of high expectations, student motivation and instructional supports in schools and classrooms.* Retrieved from http://publications.sreb.org/2012/12V03Newsletter3.pdf

Stalvey, S., & Brasell, H. (2006). Using stress balls to focus the attention of sixth grade learners. *The Journal of At-risk Issues, 12*(2), 7–16.

STAR. (2013). *California Standardized Tests.* Retrieved from http://www.startest.org/cst.html

Stockall, N.S., Dennis, L., & Miller, M. (2012). Right from the start: Universal design for preschool. *TEACHING Exceptional Children, 45*(1), 10–17.

Success for All. (2012). *Cooperative learning.* Retrieved from http://www.successforall.org/Elementary/Powerful-Instruction/Our-Instructional-Design/Cooperative-Learning/

Tarita-Nistor, L., Lam, D., Brent, M.H., Steinbach, M.J., & Gonzalez, E.G. (2013). Courier: A better font for reading with age-related macular degeneration. *Canadian Journal of Ophthalmology, 48*(1), 56–62.

Thoma, C.A., Bartholomew, C.C., & Scott, L.A. (2009). *Universal design for transition: A roadmap for planning and instruction.* Baltimore, MD: Paul H. Brookes Publishing Co.

Tomlinson, C.A. (2003). *Fulfilling the promise of the differentiated classroom: Strategies and tools for responsive teaching.* Alexandria, VA: Association for Supervision and Curriculum Development.

Tomlinson, C.A., & McTighe, J. (2006). *Integrating differentiated instruction and understanding by design: Connecting content and kids.* Alexandria, VA: Association for Supervision and Curriculum Development.

Valerie, L.M., & Foss-Swanson, S. (2012). Hey! Guess what I did in school today: Using family message journals to improve student writing and strengthen the school-home partnership. *TEACHING Exceptional Children, 44*(3), 40–48.

Vygotsky, L. (1978). *Mind in society: The development of higher psychological processes.* Cambridge, MA: Harvard University Press.

Wanzer, M.B. (2002). Use of humor in the classroom: The good, the bad, and the not-so-funny things teachers say and do. *College Teaching, 52*(1), 14–20.

Wehmeyer, M., & Schwartz, M. (1997). Self-determination and positive adult outcomes: A follow-up study of youth with mental retardation or learning disabilities. *Exceptional Children, 63*(2), 245–255.

Wiggins, G.P., & McTighe, J. (2005). *Understanding by design* (2nd ed.). Alexandria, VA: Association for Supervision and Curriculum Development.

Willingham, D. (2005, Summer). *Do visual, auditory, and kinesthetic learners need visual, auditory, and kinesthetic instruction?* Retrieved from http://www.aft.org/news pubs/periodicals/ae/summer2005/willingham.cfm

Willis, J. (2006). *Research-based strategies to ignite student learning.* Alexandria, VA: Association for Supervision and Curriculum Development.

Willis, J. (2012, January 16). *Three strategies for using the arts to build student executive functions (Part 5 of 7).* Retrieved from http://www.edutopia.org/blog/strategies-executive-functions-arts-judy-willis

Wong, H.K., & Wong, R.T. (1998). *The first days of school: How to be an effective teacher.* Mountain View, CA: Harry K. Wong Publications.

Woodcock, R.W., McGrew, K.S., & Maher, N. (2003). *Woodcock-Johnson III Normative Update (NU) Tests of Achievement.* Rolling Meadows, IL: Riverside Publishing.

Wormeli, R. (2006). *Fair isn't always equal: Assessing and grading in the differentiated classroom.* Portland, ME: Stenhouse Publishers.

Wormeli, R. (2007). *Differentiation: From planning to practice grades 6–12.* Portland, ME: Stenhouse Publishers.

Yearns, M.H. (2004, May). *Universal design for better living: Everyday tools for everyday tasks.* Retrieved from Iowa State University web site: http://www.extension .iastate.edu/NR/rdonlyres/D1D8781D-0EA2-46D0-81D6-DE90DBCAD237/96870/HandoutBetter1.pdf

Zawitz, R.X. (2009). *Learning with Tangle Brain Tools: The playful path to meaningful learning at home and in school.* San Francisco, CA: Tangle Creations.

# Index

Page numbers followed by *f* indicate figures.